Problems Solved
for the Over 50s

Prentice Hall
is an imprint of

PEARSON

Harlow, England • London • New York
Tokyo • Seoul • Taipei • New Delhi • Ca

PEARSON EDUCATION LIMITED

Edinburgh Gate
Harlow CM20 2JE
Tel: +44 (0)1279 623623
Fax: +44 (0)1279 431059
Website: www.pearsoned.co.uk

First published in Great Britain in 2011

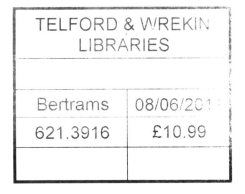

© Joli Ballew 2011

The right of Joli Ballew to be identified as author of this work has been asserted by her in accordance with the Copyright, Designs and Patents Act 1988.

Pearson Education is not responsible for the content of third party internet sites.

ISBN: 978-0-273-74635-5

British Library Cataloguing-in-Publication Data
A catalogue record for this book is available from the British Library

Library of Congress Cataloging-in-Publication Data
Ballew, Joli.
   Computer problems solved for the over 50s / Joli Ballew.
        p. cm. -- (In simple steps)
    ISBN 978-0-273-74635-5 (pbk.)
  1. Software maintenance. 2. Computers--Maintenance and repair. I. Title. II. Series.

   QA76.76.S64B355 2011
   005.1'6--dc22
                                    2011008179

Microsoft screen shots reprinted with permission from Microsoft Corporation

10 9 8 7 6 5 4 3 2 1
15 14 13 12 11

Designed by pentacorbig, High Wycombe
Typeset in 11/14 pt ITC Stone Sans by 3
Printed and bound in Great Britain by Scotprint, Haddington

Computer Problems Solved
for the Over 50s

in Simple steps

Joli Ballew

Use your computer with confidence

Get to grips with practical computing tasks with minimal time, fuss and bother.

In Simple Steps guides guarantee immediate results. They tell you everything you need to know on a specific application; from the most essential tasks to master, to every activity you'll want to accomplish, through to solving the most common problems you'll encounter.

Helpful features

To build your confidence and help you to get the most out of your computer, practical hints, tips and shortcuts feature on every page:

 ALERT: Explains and provides practical solutions to the most commonly encountered problems

 HOT TIP: Time and effort saving shortcuts

 SEE ALSO: Points you to other related tasks and information

 DID YOU KNOW? Additional features to explore

WHAT DOES THIS MEAN?
Jargon and technical terms explained in plain English

Practical. Simple. Fast.

in Simple steps

Dedication:

Mom, it's been almost two years. We all miss you deeply.

Acknowledgements:

Pearson and I go way back. I'm starting to feel like part of a family. If I'm not mistaken, this is our 13th or 14th book together in fewer than five years, and I am very proud of the relationships we fostered during that time. It's been an amazing run with lots of opportunities and successes for us all.

I would like to thank Steve Temblett, Katy Robinson and Natasha Whelan for guiding me through this book. They are all thoughtful, kind and great leaders, and let me do just about anything I want to do and in almost any time frame. I couldn't ask for any better publishing team.

As my faithful readers know, I have a family to thank, too. I have my Dad, Cosmo, Jennifer and Andrew, and a few others who are related in various ways through them. My mom passed away in February of 2009, and while expected, it hit me harder than I thought it would. Everyone recovers from such tragedies though, and generally we end up stronger for it in the end. I can say that's true for me, as I have grown intellectually and spiritually, and am faster to forgive and slower to anger. Mom would be proud. I wish she were here to see how I've grown and how well I'm taking care of Dad (who turned 90 in 2010).

I am also thankful for Neil Salkind PhD of the Salkind Literary Agency. He is my agent, but he is also my friend and mentor. Sure, he and his team read my contracts and manage my minor disputes and complaints, they watch my royalty statements and payments, and Neil secures books deals and does all of the other things you'd expect from an agent, but he's much more than that: he's a friend. We'll be celebrating ten years together in 2011, during which we've published 40 or so books. That's a long time in agent–writer years.

Finally, thanks to you, my favourite over 50s reader. May you find this book helpful and easy to understand, and I sincerely hope it assists you in resolving every computer problem you have now or will come across later. My door is an open one though. Feel free to contact me any time at joli_ballew@hotmail.com and be assured I'll write you back. I love to hear from my readers.

Publisher's acknowledgements

We are grateful to the following for permission to reproduce copyright material:

Screenshots on page 27, page 66 from Audible.com, with permission from Audible, Inc; Screenshot on page 30 from Netgear wireless broadband router DG834G, http://www.netgear.co.uk/wireless_adslrouter_dg834g.php, with permission from NETGEAR; Screenshots on page 58, page 67 from www.hp.com, Copyright 2011 Hewlett-Packard Development Company, L.P. Reproduced with permission; Screenshots on page 103, page 104, page 111 from Skype, www.skype.com, with permission from Skype Limited; Screenshots on page 110, page 150 from Adobe Reader 9.4.0, Adobe product screenshots reprinted with permission from Adobe Systems Incorporated; Screenshots on page 161 from STOPzilla, http://www.stopzilla.com, with permission from iS3, Inc; Screenshot on page 163 from http://www.symantec.com, with permission from Symantec.

Microsoft screenshots are used with permission from Microsoft Corporation.

In some instances we have been unable to trace the owners of copyright material, and we would appreciate any information that would enable us to do so.

Contents at a glance

Contents

3 Free up hard drive space

4 Fix hardware problems

8 Install missing and must-have applications

9 Resolve email problems

13 Manage and share data

14 Fix problems with media

15 Manage and maintain your PC

16 Install hardware to improve performance

Top 10 computer problems solved

Top 10 computer problems tips

Tip 1: Set a password

You can avoid a lot of problems by configuring a password for your computer. A password, if it's not easy to guess, will keep out nosy children, download-happy grandchildren and even nosy house guests! You should set a password and use the Log off feature regularly to keep your computer safe.

1 Click Start.

2 In the Start Search window, type password.

3 In the results, click Change your Windows password.

4 Click Create a password for your account.

5 Type the new password information as requested.

6 Click Create Password.

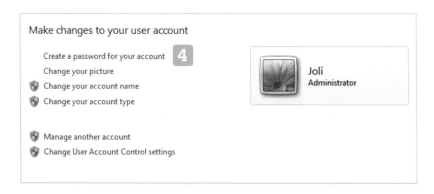

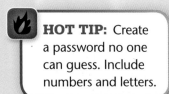 **HOT TIP:** Create a password no one can guess. Include numbers and letters.

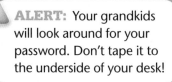 **ALERT:** Your grandkids will look around for your password. Don't tape it to the underside of your desk!

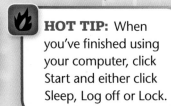 **HOT TIP:** When you've finished using your computer, click Start and either click Sleep, Log off or Lock.

Tip 2: Uninstall unwanted software

You can recoup hard drive space by uninstalling programs you no longer use, such as e-book readers, genealogy programs, gardening software and similar applications. Uninstalling these programs also helps reduce the chance that they will run in the background and use system resources.

1 Click Start and click Control Panel.

2 Click Uninstall a program.

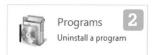

Programs
Uninstall a program

3 Select a program you no longer need. Do not select anything you do not recognise or know its purpose.

4 Click Uninstall/Change or Uninstall, whichever is offered.

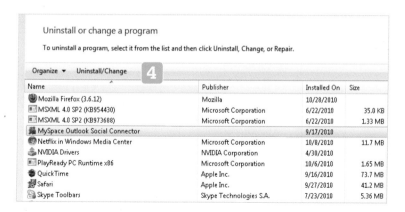

Uninstall or change a program

To uninstall a program, select it from the list and then click Uninstall, Change, or Repair.

Organize ▼   Uninstall/Change   **4**

Name	Publisher	Installed On	Size
Mozilla Firefox (3.6.12)	Mozilla	10/28/2010	
MSXML 4.0 SP2 (KB954430)	Microsoft Corporation	6/22/2010	35.0 KB
MSXML 4.0 SP2 (KB973688)	Microsoft Corporation	6/22/2010	1.33 MB
MySpace Outlook Social Connector		9/17/2010	
Netflix in Windows Media Center	Microsoft Corporation	10/8/2010	11.7 MB
NVIDIA Drivers	NVIDIA Corporation	4/30/2010	
PlayReady PC Runtime x86	Microsoft Corporation	10/6/2010	1.65 MB
QuickTime	Apple Inc.	9/16/2010	73.7 MB
Safari	Apple Inc.	9/27/2010	41.2 MB
Skype Toolbars	Skype Technologies S.A.	7/23/2010	5.36 MB

5 Work through the wizard. Each wizard is different.

6 You may be prompted when the process is complete.

MySpace for Outlook Uninstall

Uninstallation Complete
Uninstall was completed successfully.   **6**   myspace for outlook

Completed

Show details

▶ **SEE ALSO:** To see how large your hard drive is and how much free space you have, refer to Chapter 1.

? **DID YOU KNOW?**
Even if a program uses zero hard drive space, as shown, you can still benefit in other ways from uninstalling it.

Tip 3: Run the System Configuration utility

Lots of programs and applications start when you boot your computer. This causes the start-up process to take longer than it should and programs that start also run in the background, slowing down computer performance. You should disable unwanted start-up items to improve all-round performance.

1 Open the System Configuration utility. (Use the Start menu to search for it.)

2 From the Startup tab, deselect third-party programs you recognise but do not use daily.

3 Click OK.

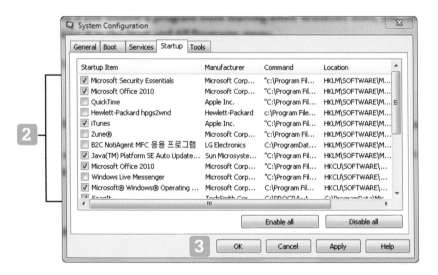

! ALERT: Do not deselect anything you don't recognise or the operating system!

! ALERT: You'll have to restart the computer to apply the changes.

? DID YOU KNOW?
Even if you disable a program from starting when Windows does, you can start it when you need it by clicking it in the Start and All Programs menu.

HOT TIP: If you see a long list under the System Configuration's Startup tab, go through it carefully and consider uninstalling unwanted programs from the Control Panel. See Chapter 3 for more information.

Tip 4: Improve performance with ReadyBoost

RAM is the place where information is stored temporarily, such as data acquired by a scanner during the scan process, or data that is calculated when you (or an application) perform tasks that require calculations. When RAM is full the data stored there is swapped to the hard drive, which is much slower than RAM. You can add space for this temporary data by incorporating ReadyBoost.

1 Insert a USB flash drive, thumb drive, portable music player or memory card into an available slot on the outside of your PC.

2 Wait while Windows 7 checks to see whether the device can perform as memory.

3 If prompted to use the flash drive or memory card to improve system performance, click Speed up my system.

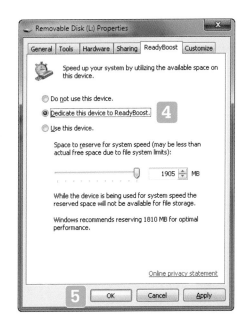

4 If you don't need the drive for data storage, opt to Dedicate this device to ReadyBoost. Otherwise, choose Use this device and allot the desired amount of space.

5 Click OK.

? DID YOU KNOW?

Only newer and larger USB keys will work for ReadyBoost. Don't worry though, you'll be informed if your device won't work.

Tip 5: Add an external hard drive

Sometimes your hardware problem is that you've run out of space on your hard drive. It's probably caused by too many videos of your grandkids! A related problem occurs when you need to back up data but your small thumb (flash) drive isn't large enough. You can resolve both of these problems and create an outstanding place to store backups for the long term by adding an external hard drive.

1 Purchase an external hard drive.

2 Follow the directions for connecting it.

3 Turn it on and wait for Windows to detect it.

4 Click Start and click Computer.

5 Note the new hard drive in the Computer window.

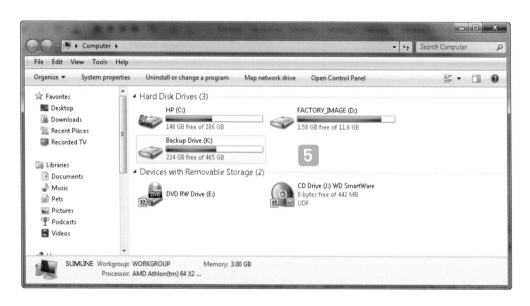

? DID YOU KNOW?

If you have another computer you don't use often, you can connect it with a network or a null-modem cable and store your backups there.

🔥 HOT TIP: Double-click the backup drive to open it, and open any other window. You can now drag and drop files from your computer to the backup drive to back them up.

Tip 6: Review sharing settings

In order for other users to be able to see your network and access the data and resources you've made available on it, you must enable Network Discovery. Once Network Discovery is enabled, you can tweak how you'd like to share those resources and with whom.

1 Open the Network and Sharing Center and click Change advanced sharing settings.

2 Your network must be visible. Verify network discovery is enabled.

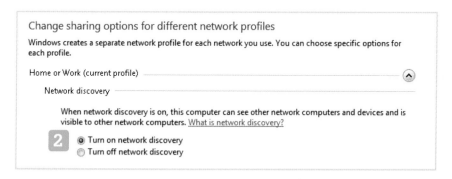

3 To share printers and data, file and printer sharing must be enabled and/or public sharing.

4 Explore other sharing options, specifically password-protected sharing.

5 Click Save changes if applicable.

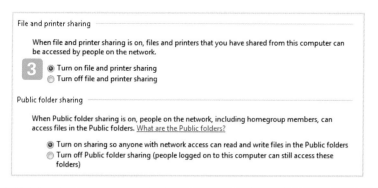

? DID YOU KNOW?

If you disable network discovery, potential users (and networked computers) won't even be able to see your network, much less join it.

Tip 7: Create a homegroup

If you have more than one Windows 7 computer on your home network, you can create a homegroup. Homegroups make sharing data, music, pictures, video and the like easier, because the homegroup configures the required settings for you.

1 Open the Network and Sharing Center.

2 Next to HomeGroup, click Ready to create. (A homegroup may have already been created and you may see something different.)

3 Click Create a homegroup (not shown).

4 Select what to share and click Next.

5 Write down the password so you can join the homegroup from your other Windows 7 networked PCs.

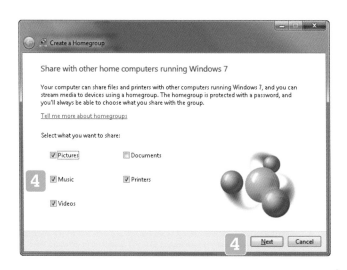

? DID YOU KNOW?
You may have created a homegroup when you set up Windows 7.

! ALERT: You can create a homegroup only if your network type is set to Home. (Work and Public won't do.)

Tip 8: Get Windows Live Essentials

Windows Live Essentials contains all of the programs you'll need to manage email, instant message with contacts, edit photos and even create and edit your own movies. You can choose to install additional applications from the suite too, including the Internet Explorer toolbar that connects all of this together seamlessly.

1 Open your web browser and navigate to
http://download.live.com/.

2 Look for the Download now button and click it. You'll be prompted to click Download now once more on the next screen.

3 Click Run and when prompted, click Yes.

4 When prompted, select the items to download. You can select all of the items or only some of them. (Make sure to at least select Live Mail, Live Messenger and Live Photo Gallery.)

5 Click Install and when prompted, select the default settings.

Download 2

System requirements

Programs you can download include:

Messenger
Mail
Writer
Photo Gallery
Movie Maker
Family Safety
Toolbar

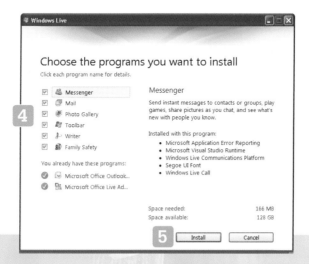

 ALERT: In Chapter 9, 'Resolve email problems', we'll be discussing Windows Live Mail.

 HOT TIP: Windows Live Essentials can be trusted to be compatible and work well.

Tip 9: Enable the Guest account

When you have guests, they may ask to use your computer to email, upload and print pictures, write and print letters, and perform other tasks. To protect your data and keep the computer safe from unintentional harm, enable the Guest account while you have a visitor.

1 Click Start and click Control Panel.

2 Click Add or remove user accounts.

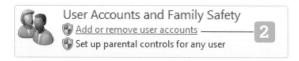

User Accounts and Family Safety
Add or remove user accounts — **2**
Set up parental controls for any user

3 Click Guest.

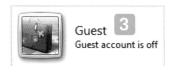

Guest **3**
Guest account is off

4 Click Turn On.

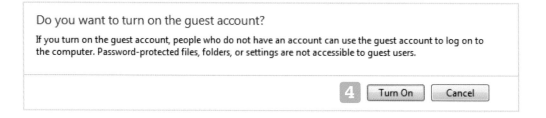

Do you want to turn on the guest account?

If you turn on the guest account, people who do not have an account can use the guest account to log on to the computer. Password-protected files, folders, or settings are not accessible to guest users.

4 [Turn On] [Cancel]

? DID YOU KNOW?

Guests who log on using the Guest account can't do anything that would harm the computer, but they can save data, use programs you've installed, surf the internet and more.

! ALERT: Disable the Guest account immediately after your guests leave. It can be a security loophole for hackers.

Tip 10: Share media from Media Player

If you want to access media on one computer from another computer on your network, you have to tell Windows 7 you want to share it. You should verify this in two places: in Media Player and in the Network and Sharing Center. The latter is detailed in Chapter 7.

1 Open Media Player from the Start, All Programs menu.

2 Click the arrow next to Stream.

3 Tick Automatically allow devices to play my media.

4 Click Automatically allow all computers and devices (not shown).

5 Repeat steps 2–4 and click Allow remote control of my Player.

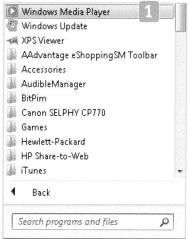

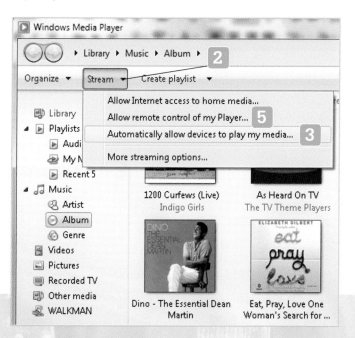

HOT TIP: Open the Network and Sharing Center, click Change advanced sharing settings and verify that Media streaming is turned on (for good measure).

SEE ALSO: Chapter 7, 'Review sharing settings'.

1 Know your computer

Introduction

This entire book is dedicated to helping you solve computer problems. You'll learn to fix hardware and software problems, resolve error messages, repair network problems and more. In order to resolve these problems though, you'll need to know where to find information about your computer. This is even more important if you ask someone else to help you. You need to know what operating system you use, how much RAM you have and how much hard drive space is available.

After you've familiarised yourself with your specific system, you'll learn what programs are running all the time, what (if any) hardware is causing system problems and what programs are installed and available for use. Finally, you'll put a few safeguards in place, just in case something happens later. You'll learn how to create a password reset disk and a system repair disk, both of which can be used to get you out of a bind if need be.

Explore your system

Your computer has lots of components. It has RAM for storing data temporarily, a hard drive for storing data long term and an operating system. There are other things too: a motherboard inside the computer, a mouse, a computer monitor and other hardware. Take a look at the devices you have to get a basic inventory.

1 Click the Start orb (from now on, I'll just say Click Start).

2 Right-click Computer and click Properties.

3 Note your Windows edition. This is your operating system.

4 Note the installed memory (this is RAM).

5 Note the system type.

? DID YOU KNOW?

Your computer's operating system is probably Windows XP, Windows Vista or Windows 7. Windows 7 is the newest edition. Windows XP is the oldest (in this list).

🔥 HOT TIP: Don't worry if you don't fully understand what you see here. You only need to know where to find the information should it ever come up in conversation, on a tech support phone call, or when checking an application's compatibility.

⚠ ALERT: When you buy software, make sure it's compatible with your Windows edition and system type, and that you have enough RAM to meet the minimum requirements.

Find your Windows Experience Index

You may have noticed *Windows Experience Index* in the previous section. This is a rating system that tells you how powerful your system is and where any weaknesses are. You can learn a lot about your system there, including how to improve performance overall.

1 Open the System window as detailed in the previous section.

2 Click Windows Experience Index.

3 Click What do these numbers mean?

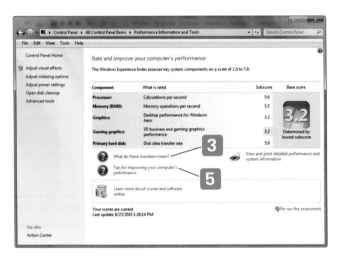

4 Read the information offered to learn how to improve performance and then close the window.

5 Click Tips for improving your computer's performance.

6 Read the information offered to learn how to improve performance and then close the window.

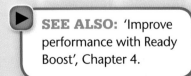 **SEE ALSO:** 'Improve performance with Ready Boost', Chapter 4.

ALERT: Do not install any internal hardware unless you're sure you know what you're doing. You can easily damage sensitive internal parts and harm your computer.

Calculate free hard drive space

A hard drive is usually a spinning disk inside your computer. You can't see it, although you might hear it whirring occasionally (if your hearing is still good!). The hard drive is where you save your letters, email, tax information, pictures and similar data. It's also where the programs you install are stored.

1 Click Start and click Computer (not shown).

2 Right-click the C: drive and click Properties.

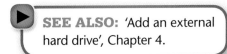 **SEE ALSO:** 'Add an external hard drive', Chapter 4.

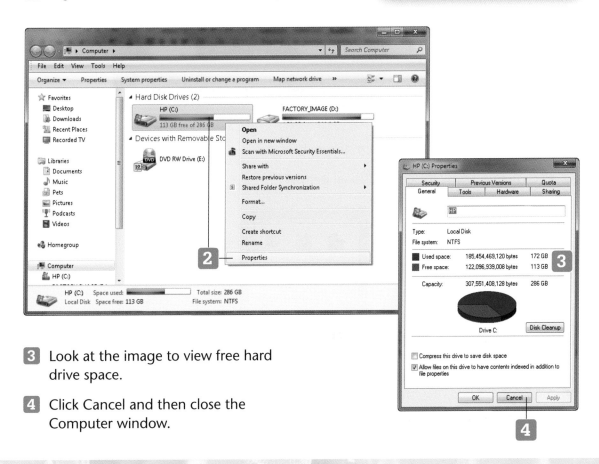

3 Look at the image to view free hard drive space.

4 Click Cancel and then close the Computer window.

ALERT: If you run low on hard drive space, you'll get a message saying so. If that happens you must delete some of the data on your hard drive to make room for new data. See Chapter 3.

HOT TIP: Although there are no hard and fast rules, I suggest you try to keep about a third of your hard drive free.

Explore programs listed in the Notification area

The taskbar's Notification area shows what programs are running in the background. These programs constantly use system resources and can slow down your computer. Closing these programs will free up the resources they are using and help performance. Alternatively, you can stop a program from booting with Windows by running the System Configuration tool, detailed in Chapter 2.

1 Locate the Notification area of the taskbar.

2 Hover your mouse over any item to see its name.

3 Click the up arrow to see additional items.

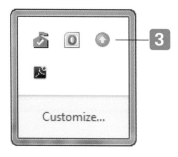

4 Hover your mouse over these as well.

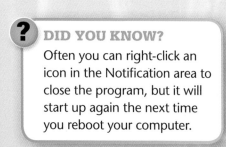

? DID YOU KNOW?
Often you can right-click an icon in the Notification area to close the program, but it will start up again the next time you reboot your computer.

🔥 HOT TIP: You should see only icons for programs you use multiple times a day here, along with items such as speakers, network, and the time and date. You should see an icon for your anti-virus software, too.

Explore your hardware in Device Manager

Using Device Manager is like getting an MRI. Your whole system is scanned and problems are reported back to you. If you make a hardware change, that change is reflected in the next scan. You can use Device Manager to uncover problems you may not know you have, just like an MRI!

1 Click Start.

2 In the Start Search window, type Device Manager.

3 Click Device Manager in the results.

4 Hopefully, you won't see any problems, as shown here.

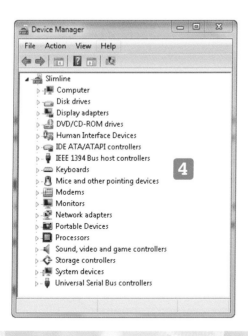

! **ALERT:** Device Manager will show red Xs and yellow exclamation points if something is wrong with a piece of hardware. If you see these, make a note and refer to the appropriate chapter in this book to resolve the issues.

? **DID YOU KNOW?**
Here the view is 'By Type'. If your screen doesn't look like this, click the View tab to change it.

Explore the All Programs menu

The Start menu offers the All Programs menu. This shows you what programs are available on your computer. If you find, after looking at the items here, that you have lots of programs you don't want or need, you should uninstall those programs to free up hard drive space and to keep the programs from using other system resources.

1 Click Start.

2 Click All Programs.

3 Use the scroll bar to review what's here.

4 You may find programs you use often, such as Microsoft Office.

5 You may find programs you don't use, ever, like software for a mobile phone you no longer own.

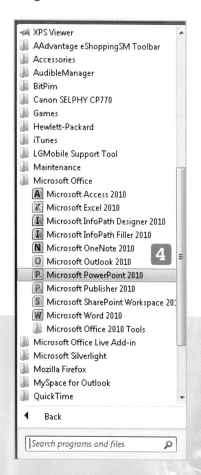

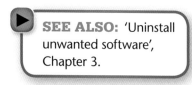

SEE ALSO: 'Uninstall unwanted software', Chapter 3.

HOT TIP: If you see an uninstall option in the All Programs menu for a program you do not want or need, you can click it to immediately uninstall it.

Create a password reset disk

Hopefully you have a password set on your user account which you have to type in each time you boot your computer or log off and back on again. If you forget this password though, you're in big trouble. And since forgetfulness is a big part of being over 50, it's better to be safe than sorry. You can create a password reset disk should this ever happen to you.

1 Click Start and type Password Reset.

2 Click Create a password reset disk in the results.

3 Read the information and click Next.

4 Choose the location to store the password key. Click Next.

5 Type your current password and click Next.

6 Click Next and Finish.

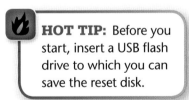

Control Panel (6)

Create a password reset disk 2

Set screen saver password

Change your Windows password

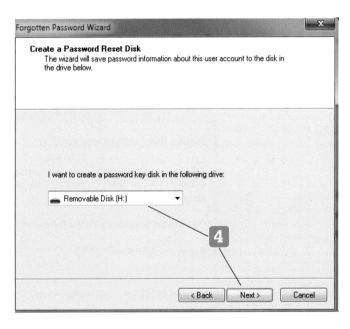

Forgotten Password Wizard

Create a Password Reset Disk
The wizard will save password information about this user account to the disk in the drive below.

I want to create a password key disk in the following drive:

Removable Disk (H:)

4

< Back | Next > | Cancel

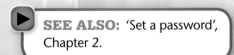

HOT TIP: Before you start, insert a USB flash drive to which you can save the reset disk.

SEE ALSO: 'Set a password', Chapter 2.

ALERT: Anyone can reset your password with the password reset disk, so keep it in a safe place.

Create a system repair disk

If your computer won't boot, you have lots of options. You can boot to Safe Mode, Last Known Good, and you can even boot with the operating system's installation DVD. Chapter 6 covers this and more. You can create your own system repair disk though, to offer yourself another option should the need arise. Again, better safe than sorry, I always say!

1 Click Start.

2 In the Start Search window, type System Repair Disc.

3 Click Create a System Repair Disc in the results.

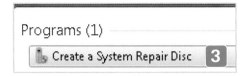

4 Select your CD/DVD rewriteable drive and click Create Disc.

5 Read the information offered and click Close, then OK.

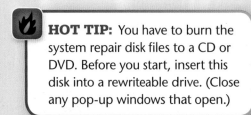

HOT TIP: You have to burn the system repair disk files to a CD or DVD. Before you start, insert this disk into a rewriteable drive. (Close any pop-up windows that open.)

ALERT: Remember to label the disk. I prefer to label with a black permanent marker.

2 First steps and quick fixes

Introduction

There are a few things you need to do right away if you've yet to do them. You need to secure your computer with a password, run Windows Update and see whether other programs have updates available. You also need to know about some Windows 7 features that watch out for problems on their own, such as the Action Center and Windows Defender. All of these things help prevent problems that would occur were you (and Windows) not so vigilant.

Even with all of this in place though, you'll still eventually encounter problems. However, there are a lot of quick fixes you can apply easily. You can reboot the computer and your network, restart hardware and update a driver. There's a built-in utility to replace missing system files, tools for disabling problematic programs, a way to turn back time, and wizards to help you with everything else. When you have a problem, any problem, this is the place to start.

Set a password

You can avoid a lot of problems by configuring a password for your computer. A password, if it's not easy to guess, will keep out nosy children, download-happy grandchildren and even nosy house guests! You should set a password and use the Log off feature regularly to keep your computer safe.

1 Click Start.

2 In the Start Search window, type password.

3 In the results, click Change your Windows password.

4 Click Create a password for your account.

5 Type the new password information as requested.

6 Click Create Password.

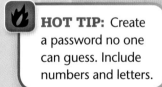 **HOT TIP:** Create a password no one can guess. Include numbers and letters.

ALERT: Your grandkids will look around for your password. Don't tape it to the underside of your desk!

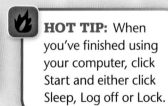 **HOT TIP:** When you've finished using your computer, click Start and either click Sleep, Log off or Lock.

Run Windows Update

Windows Update offers the easiest way to ensure your computer is as up to date as possible, at least as far as patching security flaws Microsoft uncovers, having access to the latest features and obtaining updates to the operating system itself. You should verify it's up and running.

1 Click Start.

2 Click Control Panel.

3 Click System and Security.

4 Click Windows Update.

5 In the left pane, click Change settings.

6 Configure the settings as shown here and click OK.

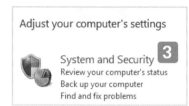

Adjust your computer's settings

System and Security **3**
Review your computer's status
Back up your computer
Find and fix problems

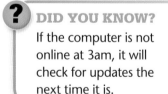

Control Panel Home

Check for updates

Change settings **5**

View update history

Restore hidden updates

Updates: frequently asked questions

Choose how Windows can install updates

When your computer is online, Windows can automatically check for important updates and install them using these settings. When new updates are available, you can also install them before shutting down the computer.
How does automatic updating help me?

Important updates

Install updates automatically (recommended)

Install new updates: Every day   at   3:00 AM

Recommended updates

☑ Give me recommended updates the same way I receive important updates

Who can install updates

6 ☑ Allow all users to install updates on this computer

Microsoft Update

☑ Give me updates for Microsoft products and check for new optional Microsoft software when I update Windows

Software notifications

☐ Show me detailed notifications when new Microsoft software is available

Note: Windows Update might update itself automatically first when checking for other updates. Read our privacy statement online.

6 OK   Cancel

? **DID YOU KNOW?**
If the computer is not online at 3am, it will check for updates the next time it is.

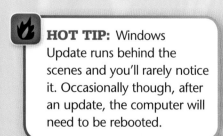

HOT TIP: Windows Update runs behind the scenes and you'll rarely notice it. Occasionally though, after an update, the computer will need to be rebooted.

! ALERT: You may see that optional components or updates are available. You can view these updates and install them if desired.

Update third-party programs

Windows Update helps you keep your operating system up to date with the latest security fixes and newest features. Generally, software manufacturers offer updates regularly too, just like Microsoft does. Often though, these updates aren't 'pushed' to your machine like Windows updates are – you have to check for updates yourself.

1 Click Start, click All Programs and open a program you use regularly.

2 If there's a Help menu, click it.

3 Look for and click Check for Update, or something similar.

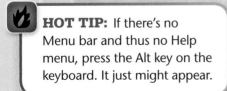 **HOT TIP:** If there's no Menu bar and thus no Help menu, press the Alt key on the keyboard. It just might appear.

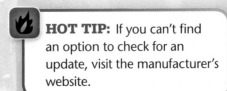 **HOT TIP:** If you can't find an option to check for an update, visit the manufacturer's website.

Check the Action Center in Windows 7

Windows 7 tries hard to take care of your PC and your data. You'll see a pop-up if your anti-virus software is out of date (or not installed), if you don't have the proper security settings configured, or if Windows Update is disabled. When you see alerts, pay attention! You'll want to resolve them.

1 Open the Action Center.

2 If there's anything in red or yellow, click the down arrow (if necessary) to see the problem.

3 Click the suggestion button to view the resolution and perform the task. Here, that's Options.

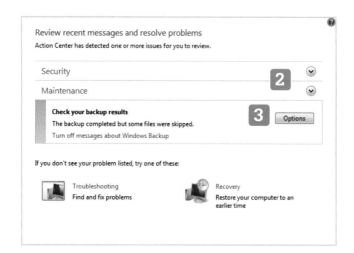

ALERT: Install anti-virus software to protect your PC from viruses and worms.

? DID YOU KNOW?
Windows 7 comes with malware protection but not anti-virus protection.

WHAT DOES THIS MEAN?

Virus: a self-replicating program that infects computers with intent to do harm. Viruses often come in the form of an attachment in an email.

Worm: a self-replicating program that infects computers with intent to do harm. However, unlike a virus, it does not need to attach itself to a running program.

Scan with Windows Defender

You don't have to do much with Windows Defender except understand that it offers protection against internet threats such as malware. It's enabled by default and it runs in the background. However, if you ever think your computer has been attacked by an internet threat (virus, worm, malware, etc.) you can run a manual scan here.

1 Open Windows Defender. (Use the Start menu to search for it.)

2 Click the arrow next to Scan (not the Scan icon). Click Full scan if you think the computer has been infected.

3 Click the X in the top right corner to close the Windows Defender window.

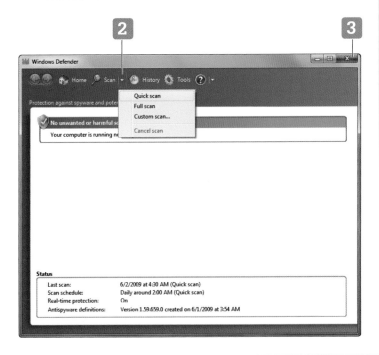

WHAT DOES THIS MEAN?

Malware: stands for malicious software. Malware includes viruses, worms, spyware, etc.

ALERT: You may be prompted after completing step 1 that Windows Defender has been turned off because you use another program to secure your computer. Do not turn Windows Defender on. Instead, use the malware program you purchased to run a scan.

Reboot the PC, modems and routers

You'll be amazed at just how often restarting your computer will resolve a problem. After rebooting, if the problem is not resolved, you can try other solutions. If your problem is that your computer cannot connect to the internet, you can reboot the computer *and* the network hardware.

1 Turn off the PC and turn off and unplug the modem and router (as applicable).

2 If the modem has a battery backup, remove the battery.

3 After a minute or so, reinsert the battery, plug in the modem, and turn it on.

4 After the modem has finished initialising, turn on the router, switch or hub.

5 After that device has finished initialising, turn on the PC.

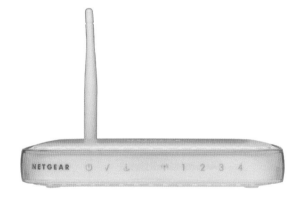

HOT TIP: The modem has finished initialising after all of its lights have stopped blinking.

SEE ALSO: Chapter 7 is all about resolving network and internet problems. However, rebooting everything is always a good first step. Refer to that chapter if this does not resolve your problem.

? DID YOU KNOW?
Often, you can disconnect, turn off and turn back on a peripheral such as a printer or scanner to resolve hardware problems quickly.

HOT TIP: Many problems occur due to loose or disconnected cables. A mouse can't work unless it's plugged in or its wireless component is. A cable modem can't work unless it's connected securely to the computer and the wall. When troubleshooting, always check your connections.

Use System Restore

System Restore regularly creates and saves *restore points* that contain information about your computer that Windows uses to work properly. If your computer starts acting strangely, you can use System Restore to restore it to a time when the computer was working properly. It's like turning back time!

1 Open System Restore. (Use the Start Search window to locate it.)

2 Click Next to accept and apply the recommended restore point.

3 Click Finish.

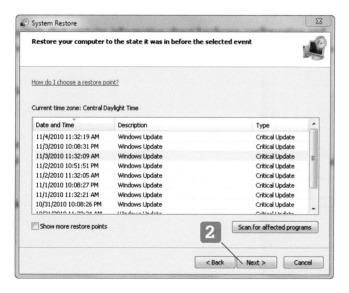

? DID YOU KNOW?
Because System Restore works only with its own system files, running System Restore will not affect any of your personal data. Your pictures, email, documents, music, etc. will not be deleted or changed.

⚠ ALERT: If running System Restore on a laptop, make sure it's plugged in. System Restore should never be interrupted.

WHAT DOES THIS MEAN?
Restore point: a snapshot of the Registry and system state that can be used to make an unstable computer stable again.
Registry: a part of the operating system that contains information about hardware configuration and settings, user configuration and preferences, software configuration and preferences, and other system-specific information.

Update a driver

A driver is a piece of software that enables computer hardware to communicate with the computer. Drivers are loaded when you install the hardware. If you're having problems with a particular piece of hardware and that hardware is listed in Device Manager, you can update its driver.

1 Open Device Manager. (Use the Start Search window to locate it.)

2 Click the small triangle next to the hardware that is currently problematic.

3 Double-click the device name.

4 Click the Driver tab and click Update Driver.

5 Click OK.

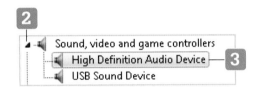

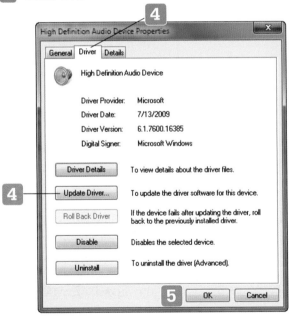

SEE ALSO: There's a slew of information about drivers in Chapter 4, 'Fix hardware problems'.

ALERT: Printers, scanners and similar hardware aren't listed in Device Manager. What is listed are devices that are required for your computer to function properly, such as mice, monitors and keyboards, and all of the internal hardware, such as CD/DVD drives, network adapters and disk drives.

Replace missing system files

Once in a blue moon you'll boot your computer and be informed that some system files are missing or can't be found. It's certainly unnerving. The good news is that there's a utility to restore those missing files. It's the System File Checker.

1 Click Start and type Command Prompt.

2 In the result, right-click Command Prompt.

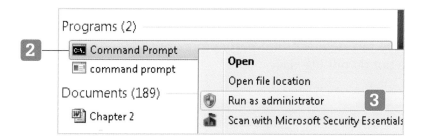

3 Click Run as administrator.

4 Input administrator credentials when prompted.

5 At the command prompt, type sfc /scannow.

6 Press Enter on the keyboard.

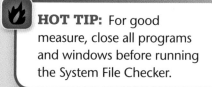

HOT TIP: For good measure, close all programs and windows before running the System File Checker.

ALERT: Do not disturb your computer while the System File Checker is running.

Run the System Configuration utility

Lots of programs and applications start when you boot your computer. This causes the start-up process to take longer than it should, and programs that start also run in the background, slowing down computer performance. You should disable unwanted start-up items to improve all-round performance.

1 Open the System Configuration utility. (Use the Start menu to search for it.)

2 From the Startup tab, deselect third-party programs you recognise but do not use daily.

3 Click OK.

Programs (1)

System Configuration **1**

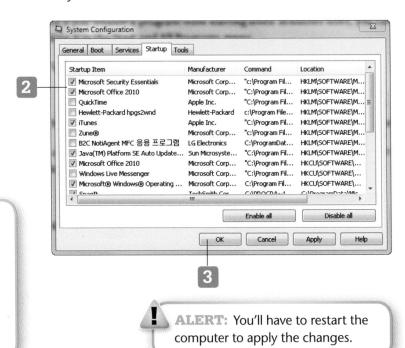

? DID YOU KNOW?
Even if you disable a program from starting when Windows does, you can start it when you need it by clicking it in the Start and All Programs menu.

! ALERT: You'll have to restart the computer to apply the changes.

🔥 HOT TIP: If you see a long list under the System Configuration's Startup tab, go through it carefully and consider uninstalling unwanted programs from the Control Panel. See Chapter 3 for more information.

! ALERT: Do not deselect anything you don't recognise or the operating system!

Locate Help

You may be able to resolve a problem quickly by following the steps outlined in Help and Support files or the Action Center. You can access the Help files from the Start menu (Start, Help and Support). You can work with the Help and Support files the same way you browse webpages. Just type in your question and peruse the solutions.

You can also use the Action Center:

1 Open the Action Center. (Use the Start menu to search for it.)

2 Click Troubleshooting.

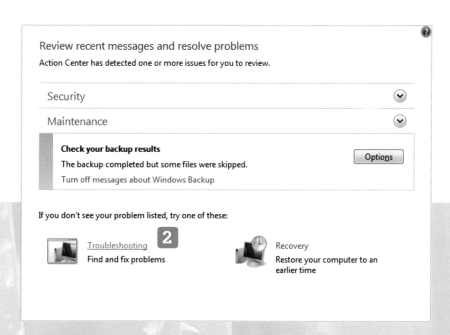

3 Select the category that details the type of problem you're having.

4 Work through the wizard to resolve the problem.

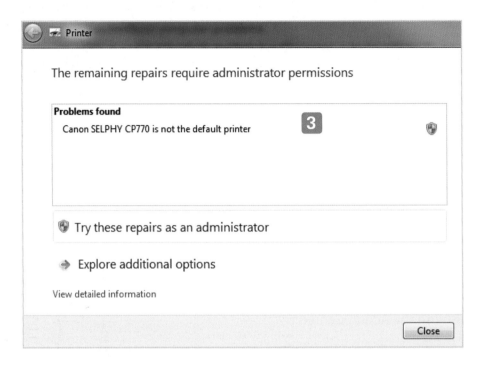

 **HOT TIP:** If you don't find what you want here quickly, flip to the appropriate chapter of this book for help. You can also get help online from http://support.microsoft.com/.

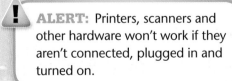 **ALERT:** Printers, scanners and other hardware won't work if they aren't connected, plugged in and turned on.

3 Free up hard drive space

Introduction

Your computer's hard drive is what stores all of your data. This includes letters you type, emails you send and receive, videos you download, pictures you acquire, and spreadsheets you create. The hard drive also holds its own stuff, including the operating system, programs, Windows updates, and data acquired by Windows Defender, the Action Center, and other areas. If you never deleted anything, but kept adding data, your hard drive might eventually get full. In this chapter you'll learn how to keep that from happening.

Delete unnecessary files and folders

You create and acquire data regularly. You save pictures of your grandkids, write letters to public officials, and create spreadsheets with the names and addresses of your team members. You may even record television shows on your computer or purchase movies and videos. There's probably some data you can delete.

1 Click Start, then click Documents.

2 If you see something you can delete:

   a. Right-click it.

   b. Click Delete.

   c. Click Yes to verify.

   d. Repeat as necessary.

3 Click Start, then click Pictures.

4 Repeat step 2.

5 Click Start, then click Music.

6 Repeat step 2.

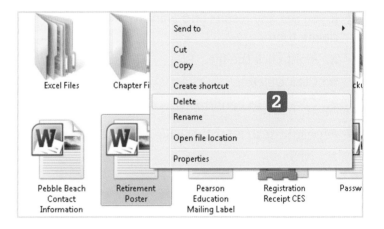

HOT TIP: If you can't see the icons very well because they are too small, look for the View button on the toolbar (two to the left of the Help button) in the Documents, Pictures or Music window to select a larger size.

Search for and delete specific file types

You may have data stored on your computer that you know is a specific file type. For instance, Photoshop files are often saved as .psd files. You may also have PDF files, XPS files and more. You can search for these files specifically from the Start menu.

1 Click Start.

2 In the Start Search window, type .pdf.

3 If you see any results and want to delete them:

    a. Right-click the file.

    b. Click Delete.

    c. Click Yes to confirm.

4 Repeat to search for these file types:

    a. .XPS

    b. .psd

    c. .gif

    d. .jpg

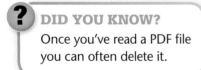

? DID YOU KNOW?

Once you've read a PDF file you can often delete it.

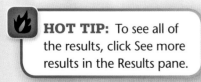

HOT TIP: To see all of the results, click See more results in the Results pane.

ALERT: There are hundreds of potential file types you could have stored on your computer. Step 4 names only a few.

Uninstall unwanted software

Another place you can recoup hard drive space is by uninstalling programs you no longer use, such as e-book readers, genealogy programs, gardening software and similar applications. Uninstalling these programs also helps reduce the chance that they will run in the background and use system resources.

1 Click Start and click Control Panel.

2 Click Uninstall a program.

Programs
Uninstall a program **2**

3 Select a program you no longer need. Do not select anything you do not recognise or know its purpose.

4 Click Uninstall/Change or Uninstall, whichever is offered.

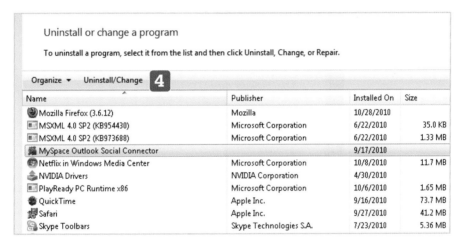

Uninstall or change a program

To uninstall a program, select it from the list and then click Uninstall, Change, or Repair.

Organize ▾   Uninstall/Change **4**

Name	Publisher	Installed On	Size
Mozilla Firefox (3.6.12)	Mozilla	10/28/2010	
MSXML 4.0 SP2 (KB954430)	Microsoft Corporation	6/22/2010	35.0 KB
MSXML 4.0 SP2 (KB973688)	Microsoft Corporation	6/22/2010	1.33 MB
MySpace Outlook Social Connector		9/17/2010	
Netflix in Windows Media Center	Microsoft Corporation	10/8/2010	11.7 MB
NVIDIA Drivers	NVIDIA Corporation	4/30/2010	
PlayReady PC Runtime x86	Microsoft Corporation	10/6/2010	1.65 MB
QuickTime	Apple Inc.	9/16/2010	73.7 MB
Safari	Apple Inc.	9/27/2010	41.2 MB
Skype Toolbars	Skype Technologies S.A.	7/23/2010	5.36 MB

5 Work through the wizard. Each wizard is different.

6 You may be prompted when the process is complete.

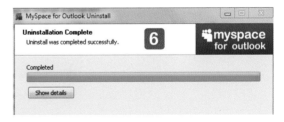

MySpace for Outlook Uninstall

Uninstallation Complete
Uninstall was completed successfully. **6**   **myspace** for outlook

Completed

Show details

SEE ALSO: To see how large your hard drive is and how much free space you have, refer to Chapter 1.

HOT TIP: Even if a program uses zero hard drive space, as shown, you can still benefit in other ways from uninstalling it.

Delete unnecessary System Restore files

System Restore, detailed in Chapter 2, saves data that is necessary to restore your computer to an earlier time, should the need ever arise. If you've tweaked the settings though, and told System Restore that you want to keep a lot of data, that data can fill up your hard drive quickly. You should check to be sure.

1 Click Start.

2 Right-click Computer and click Properties.

3 Click System protection.

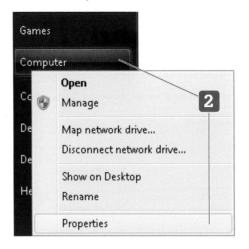

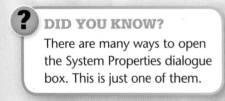

? DID YOU KNOW?

There are many ways to open the System Properties dialogue box. This is just one of them.

4 Click Configure.

5 In the resulting screen, note how much hard drive space is currently being allocated to System Restore.

6 Reposition the slider where you're comfortable. I prefer to leave it at about 20%.

7 Click OK, Yes and then OK again.

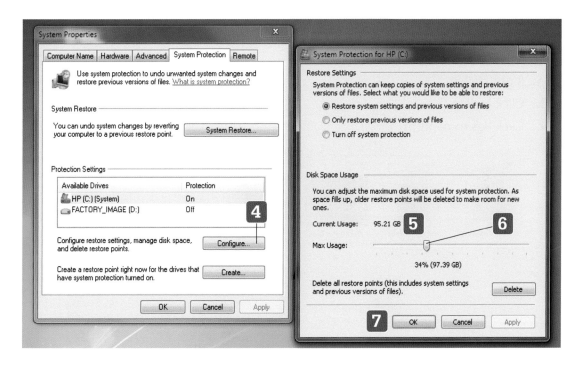

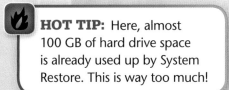
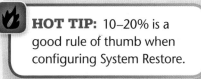

Delete unwanted media files

Media files can really fill up a hard drive fast. Pictures aren't so bad, but home videos, videos you purchase and TV you record can be space hogs. For the most part, these videos are saved in your Videos folder.

1 Click Start, then click your user name.

2 Click My Videos.

3 To delete a video:

    a. Right-click it.

    b. Click Delete.

    c. Click Yes to confirm.

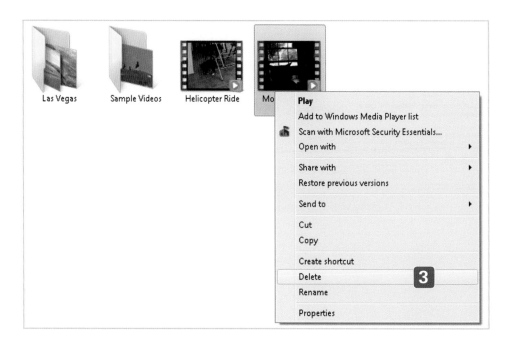

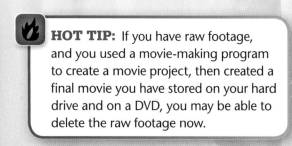

HOT TIP: If you have raw footage, and you used a movie-making program to create a movie project, then created a final movie you have stored on your hard drive and on a DVD, you may be able to delete the raw footage now.

4 Click Start and type Recorded TV.

5 Under Pictures, click Recorded TV.

6 Repeat step 2 to delete unwanted media.

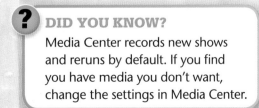

ALERT: If you find a lot of recorded TV, you need to change the record settings in Media Center.

DID YOU KNOW?
Media Center records new shows and reruns by default. If you find you have media you don't want, change the settings in Media Center.

Run Disk Cleanup

Disk Cleanup is a safe and effective way to reduce unnecessary data on your PC. With unnecessary data deleted, your PC will run faster and have more available disk space for saving files and installing programs. With Disk Cleanup you can remove temporary files, empty the Recycle Bin, remove set up log files and downloaded program files (among other things), all in a single process.

1 Click Start and search for Disk Cleanup.

2 Select Disk Cleanup in the results.

3 If prompted, choose the drive or partition to clean up. It's probably C:.

4 Click OK.

5 Place a tick by each item to clean.

6 Click OK.

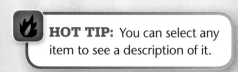

HOT TIP: You can select any item to see a description of it.

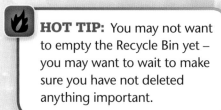

HOT TIP: You may not want to empty the Recycle Bin yet – you may want to wait to make sure you have not deleted anything important.

Empty the Recycle Bin

The Recycle Bin holds data you've deleted until you empty it. If you've deleted a lot of data in this chapter, you may want to wait a few days before emptying it. That way, if you decide you want to get something back, you can.

1 Right-click the Recycle Bin on the desktop.

2 Click Empty Recycle Bin.

3 Alternatively, you can run Disk Cleanup again and check the Recycle Bin before clicking OK.

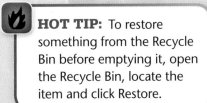

HOT TIP: To restore something from the Recycle Bin before emptying it, open the Recycle Bin, locate the item and click Restore.

ALERT: Once you delete items in the Recycle Bin there's no way to get them back, short of hiring Scotland Yard to do it!

Access Disk Defragmenter

Disk Defragmenter analyses the data stored on your hard drive and consolidates files that are not stored together. This enhances performance by enabling your hard drive to work faster by making data easier to access. Disk Defragmenter runs automatically once a week, in the middle of the night.

1 Click Start. In the Start Search dialogue box, type Defrag.

2 Under Programs, select Disk Defragmenter.

3 Verify that Disk Defragmenter is configured to run on a schedule.

4 If you want to change when Disk Defragmenter runs or schedule it to run, click Configure schedule.

5 Select a choice for Choose frequency, Choose day, Choose time and Choose disks, using the drop-down lists.

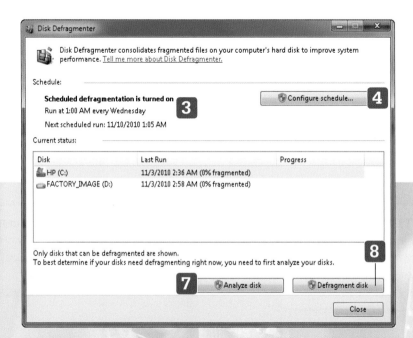

6 Click OK to close the scheduling dialogue box.

7 Click Analyze disk. Wait – this could take a while.

8 If you want to run Disk Defragmenter now, click Defragment disk. There's generally no need to do this.

9 Click OK.

Disk	Last Run	Progress
HP (C:)	11/4/2010 2:44 PM (0% fragmented)	
FACTORY_IMAGE (D:)	11/3/2010 2:58 AM (0% fragmented)	

 HOT TIP: If you know your computer won't be turned on in the middle of the night when Disk Defragmenter is set to run, configure a time for it when it will be turned on and not in use (perhaps early Sunday morning).

 HOT TIP: It's best to run Disk Defragmenter after using Disk Cleanup and after deleting a large amount of files.

 DID YOU KNOW? Once Disk Defragmenter is set to run on a schedule, you should never have to manually use or access it.

 ALERT: By default, all volumes (or hard drive partitions) are selected, so there's no need to click Select Volumes to make changes.

4 Fix hardware problems

Introduction

Most of the time, hardware problems are easily resolved. A printer is turned off and needs to be turned on, a cable has been damaged by a frisky cat or run over and damaged by a wheeled chair, a scanner has gone to 'sleep' and needs to be turned off and on again to wake it up, and media cards have been inadvertently protected by a slider that's been moved from off to on. Sometimes hardware has been plugged into a non-working electrical outlet or connected to a non-working USB port on the computer, which are two problems that it's easy to forget to check.

However, sometimes problems are more complex. Perhaps you need more RAM but don't know how to add it (or can't), or an internal component has worked its way loose and no longer works. Some hardware is simply incompatible and must be replaced, while other devices just need a new driver. We'll look at all of that here.

Understand common hardware problems

The most common problems that occur with malfunctioning hardware are listed at the beginning of this chapter. Reread that page now and make sure that the following is true before continuing your troubleshooting tasks.

- Click Start and click Devices and Printers to view connected devices. If your device is not shown:
    - Turn off the device and then turn it back on.
    - Plug the device into a different electrical outlet or replace the batteries in it.
    - Verify the USB or FireWire port is working by plugging a known working device into it.
    - Verify the cable is functional by plugging in a different device with it.
- If it's a media card or camera, make sure the card isn't protected and the camera is set to the proper mode.

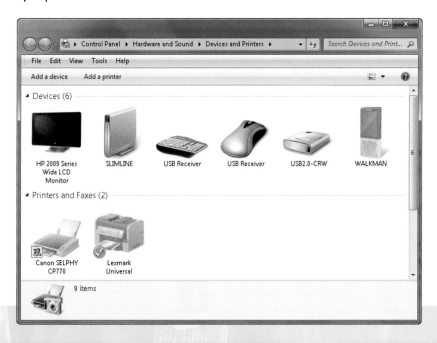

HOT TIP: Hardware such as wireless mice and keyboards will stop working when their batteries die.

HOT TIP: You can't print to a printer that's disconnected from the computer or turned off.

ALERT: If your device does not appear in the Devices and Printers window, Windows can't use it.

Verify Windows compatibility

Some hardware just isn't meant to work with Windows. Some hardware that used to work with Windows XP won't work with Windows 7. If your hardware is not compatible, and you can't find a driver to force it into submission, it's just not going to happen. You can check to see whether hardware is compatible in a number of ways.

1 Open your web browser.

2 In the Address bar type: http://www.microsoft.com/windows/compatibility/.

3 Click Hardware.

4 Enter the product name and click Search.

5 To check your entire system:

  a. Connect and turn on all external hardware.

  b. Run the Windows 7 Upgrade Advisor, available from the link above.

SEE ALSO: 'Locate a driver on the internet', later in this chapter.

HOT TIP: If you find that a device is not compatible, that doesn't mean there's no way it will ever work. Check the manufacturer's website for an updated driver – there may be one available.

Improve performance with ReadyBoost

RAM is the place where information is stored temporarily, such as data acquired by a scanner during the scan process, or data that is calculated when you (or an application) perform tasks that require calculations. When RAM is full the data stored there is swapped to the hard drive, which is much slower than RAM. You can add space for this temporary data by incorporating ReadyBoost.

1 Insert a USB flash drive, thumb drive, portable music player or memory card into an available slot on the outside of your PC.

2 Wait while Windows 7 checks to see whether the device can perform as memory.

3 If prompted to use the flash drive or memory card to improve system performance, click Speed up my system.

4 If you don't need the drive for data storage, opt to Dedicate this device to ReadyBoost. Otherwise, choose Use this device and allot the desired amount of space.

5 Click OK.

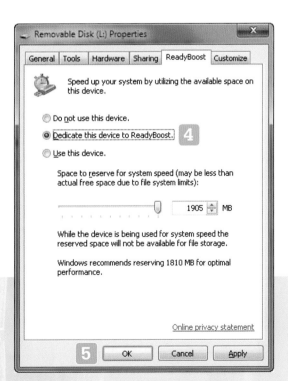

? DID YOU KNOW?

Only newer and larger USB keys will work for ReadyBoost. Don't worry though, you'll be informed if your device won't work.

WHAT DOES THIS MEAN?

ReadyBoost: a technology that lets you add hard drive cache (which acts like RAM) to a PC easily, without opening the computer tower or the laptop case.

Troubleshoot sound problems

You learned at the end of Chapter 3 that there are various wizards to help you resolve computer problems. Here, you'll use one to troubleshoot sound problems.

1 Open Action Center. (Use the Start menu to search for it.)

2 Click Troubleshooting.

3 Click Hardware and Sound (unless an option under it suits your exact needs).

4 Select the item in the list that best describes the problem you're having.

5 Work through the wizard to resolve the problem. (Here, there may be a problem with the audio jack.)

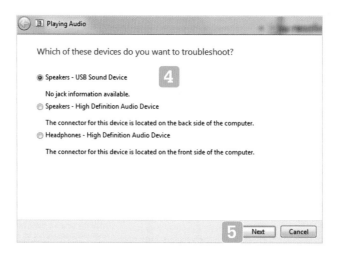

HOT TIP: Remember, you can't use a device if it's not turned on and connected, and plugged into an electrical outlet if required.

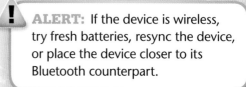

ALERT: If the device is wireless, try fresh batteries, resync the device, or place the device closer to its Bluetooth counterpart.

Troubleshoot printer problems

Here, you'll use a wizard to troubleshoot printer problems.

1 Open Action Center. (Use the Start menu to search for it.)

2 Click Troubleshooting.

3 Under Hardware and Sound, click Use a printer.

4 Click Next.

5 Select the printer you're having trouble with, or select My printer is not listed.

6 Work through the wizard to resolve the problem.

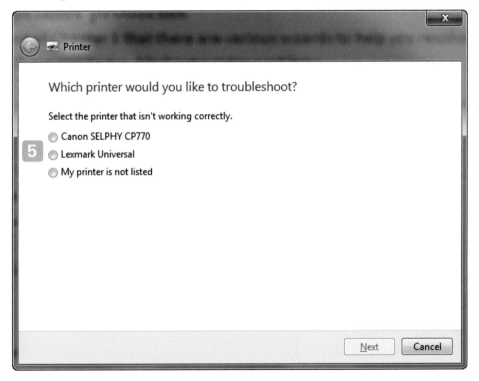

HOT TIP: Remember, you can't use a device if it's not turned on and connected, and plugged into an electrical outlet if required.

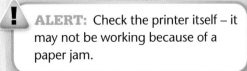

ALERT: Check the printer itself – it may not be working because of a paper jam.

Locate a driver on the internet

You know that almost all of the time, hardware installs automatically and with no input from you (other than plugging it in and turning it on). However, in rare cases, the hardware does not install properly. If this happens, and if you cannot replace the device with something Windows 7 recognises, you'll have to locate and install the driver yourself.

1 Write down the name and model number of the device (usually located on the bottom of the device).

2 Open your web browser and locate the manufacturer's website.

3 Locate a link for Support, Support & Drivers, Customer Support, or something similar. Click it.

» HP Home   » Products & Services   » Support & Drivers

» Contact HP

Copyright 2011 Hewlett-Packard Development Company, L. P. Reproduced with permission

4 Locate your device driver by make, model or other characteristics.

5 Work your way to the webpage that contains the driver.

Step two: Select a download

Additional software & driver video help

Show all | Hide all

Driver (1) 5

» HP Deskjet Printer Driver Information and Instructions
2001-10-09 , Version:1 , 19.0k

Copyright 2011 Hewlett-Packard Development Company, L. P. Reproduced with permission

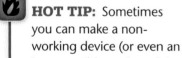 **HOT TIP:** Sometimes you can make a non-working device (or even an incompatible one) work by installing an updated driver.

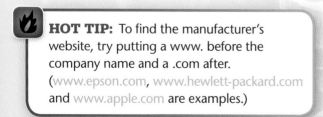 **HOT TIP:** To find the manufacturer's website, try putting a www. before the company name and a .com after. (www.epson.com, www.hewlett-packard.com and www.apple.com are examples.)

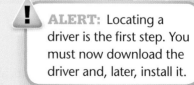 **ALERT:** Locating a driver is the first step. You must now download the driver and, later, install it.

Download and install a driver

If you've located the driver you need, you can now download and install it. Downloading is the process of saving the driver to your computer's hard drive. Once downloaded, you can install the driver.

1 Locate the driver as detailed in the previous section.

2 Click the driver link to download the driver.

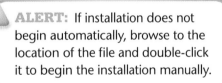

3 Click Save. Alternatively, you can click Run.

4 Click Run, Install or Open Window to begin the installation, as applicable. If you opt to open the window, you'll need to click the file to run it.

5 Follow the directions in the set-up process to complete the installation.

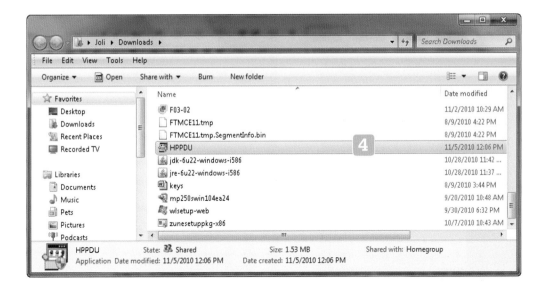

HOT TIP: Save the file in a location you recognise, such as Downloads.

ALERT: If installation does not begin automatically, browse to the location of the file and double-click it to begin the installation manually.

Rollback a bad driver

If you download and install a new driver for a piece of hardware and it doesn't work properly, you can use Device Driver Rollback to return to the previously installed driver.

1 Click Start.

2 Right-click Computer.

3 Click Properties.

4 Under Tasks, click Device Manager (not shown).

5 Click the triangle next to the hardware that uses the driver to rollback.

6 Double-click the device name.

7 Click the Driver tab and click Roll Back Driver.

8 Click Close.

Add an external hard drive

Sometimes your hardware problem is that you've run out of space on your hard drive. It's probably caused by too many videos of your grandkids! A related problem occurs when you need to back up data but your small thumb (flash) drive isn't large enough. You can resolve both of these problems and create an outstanding place to store backups for the long term by adding an external hard drive.

1 Purchase an external hard drive.

2 Follow the directions for connecting it.

3 Turn it on and wait for Windows to detect it.

4 Click Start and click Computer.

5 Note the new hard drive in the Computer window.

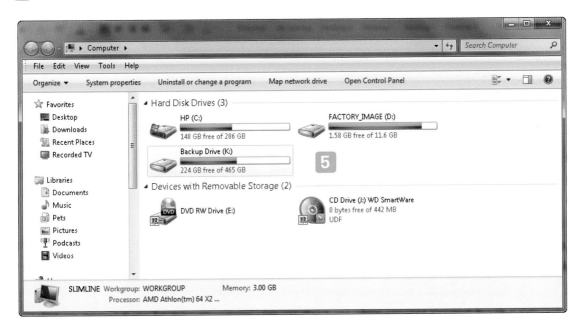

DID YOU KNOW?

If you have another computer you don't use often, you can connect it with a network or a null-modem cable and store your backups there.

HOT TIP: Double-click the backup drive to open it, and open any other window. You can now drag and drop files from your computer to the backup drive to back them up.

Reseat non-working internal hardware

In a worst-case scenario, internal hardware or the cable that connects the hardware to the motherboard becomes dislodged (or unseated). You can assume this is probably the problem if you can't see a device like a CD/DVD drive in Device Manager or if you're seeing only half of the RAM you expect to see in the Computer Properties window.

1 First, verify the device is not disabled in Device Manager. If it is, enable it.

2 Open the computer case, being careful not to touch any internal parts.

3 Ground yourself by touching a metal part of the computer case.

4 Look for dislodged or poorly seated cables or RAM.

5 Carefully reconnect them.

6 Replace the case and turn on the computer.

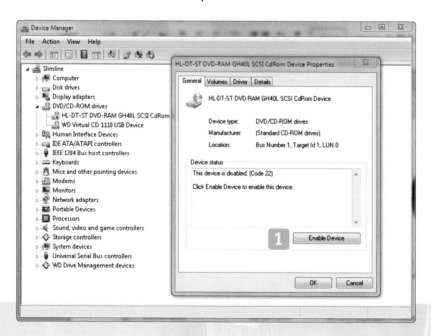

ALERT: If you have recently moved or kicked your computer and now believe that internal hardware has become disconnected, I suggest you take the computer to a repair shop.

ALERT: You can severely damage the computer if you mess something up here. Again, I heartily suggest taking the computer to a professional repair shop.

5 Fix software problems

Introduction

Software is what you install on your computer to help you perform tasks. You may install image-editing software to fix photos, office software to write letters, create greeting cards or create presentations, genealogy software to trace your family tree, or messaging software to view your grandkids on a web cam over the internet.

Sometimes, problems can occur with the software you've installed, or software that the computer manufacturer installed for you. One day you're using the software, and the next day, you aren't. There's often no rhyme or reason for it either. Problems with software occur often enough that we've dedicated an entire chapter to it. So don't worry – you're not alone!

Browse menus for Help

The first place to look for a resolution to a software problem is in the program's Help files. We've never used a program that did not come with Help files, but you may have to look hard to find them. If you can open the program, you can usually open the Help files too.

1 Open the troublesome program.

2 Click the Help menu if it is available.

3 If available, click a troubleshooting option. If not, click whatever is the next best thing.

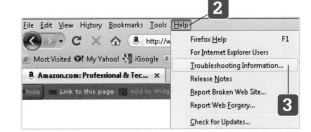

4 If no Help menu exists, press F1 on the keyboard.

5 If F1 does not offer Help files, look for a small question mark and click it.

6 Once inside the Help files, browse for a solution to your problem.

HOT TIP: Press Alt on the keyboard if you don't see any menus across the top of the program window.

HOT TIP: You can't print a file in Microsoft Office 2010 if it has been opened in Protected View. Thus, a problem that occurs because you can't print may not have anything to do with your printer but more to do with your software.

Update software

You learned in Chapter 2 that checking for updates to software can often serve as a 'quick fix' for resolving computer problems. The same is true here. Often, problems that are reported to the company that created the troublesome software are resolved via updates.

1 Click Start, click All Programs, and open a program you use regularly.

2 If there's a Help menu, click it.

3 Look for and click Check for Update, or something similar.

? DID YOU KNOW?

The terms software, program and application are often used interchangeably.

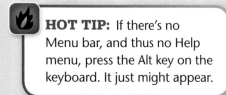

HOT TIP: If there's no Menu bar, and thus no Help menu, press the Alt key on the keyboard. It just might appear.

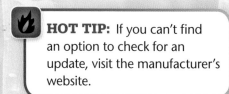

HOT TIP: If you can't find an option to check for an update, visit the manufacturer's website.

Reinstall software

If you see errors when you start or use a program, you're probably missing one or more of the files required for the program to run properly. Reinstalling the software almost always resolves problems discovered through on-screen error messages.

1 Locate the software. It may be:

    a. On a CD or DVD. Put it in the CD/DVD drive.

    b. Saved to your hard drive.

    c. On the manufacturer's website. Download the software and save it.

2 Locate the 'executable' file or Install command and click it. It may say:

    a. Setup.

    b. Install.

    c. Run.

3 Follow the prompts to run the installation program.

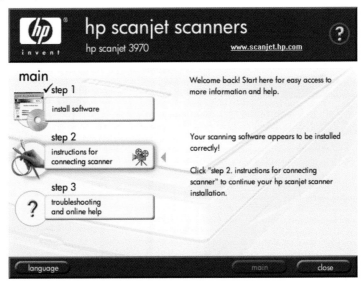

Copyright 2011 Hewlett-Packard Development Company, L. P.
Reproduced with permission

? DID YOU KNOW?

Files can go missing for a variety of reasons, and often missing files are not your fault.

? DID YOU KNOW?

Old software is often hard to find on the internet if you've lost the disk. There are a lot of shady characters out there who will try to trick you into installing something that looks like your software but isn't. If you can't find the software from the manufacturer's website, install something newer to replace it.

Run in compatibility mode

There's something called Program Compatibility Mode that enables you to run software originally created for an older operating system. This means that you can run software made for Windows XP on a Windows 7 machine, all the while tricking the software into thinking you've installed it on a much older PC than the one you use!

1 Locate the icon for the software that isn't running properly.

2 Right-click the icon and click Properties.

3 Click the Compatibility tab. (If you don't see it, you'll have to try a different icon.)

4 Click Run this program in compatibility mode for: and select an operating system (OS).

5 Click OK.

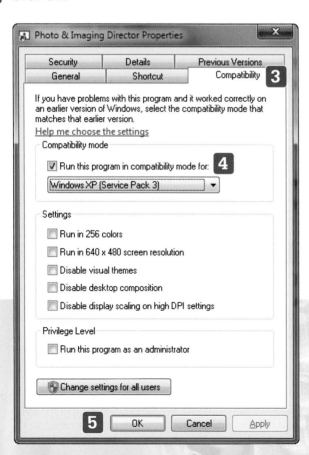

HOT TIP: Try different modes until you find the best results.

ALERT: Don't run anti-virus software in Program Compatibility Mode, it won't work as well as it should. Instead, upgrade to newer software. (Try the free Microsoft Security Essentials.)

HOT TIP: If you install an old program created for, say, Windows XP, but it doesn't run properly on Windows 7, try running it in Program Compatibility Mode.

Google error messages

If you've tried the options outlined in this chapter but are still getting error messages (or errors) when you open a specific program, you'll have to search for the solution on the internet. You search by typing in the exact error message you see.

1 Write down the error message you receive, exactly as it appears.

2 If you are experiencing a specific problem, think of a succinct way of describing it.

3 Open your web browser and go to www.google.com.

4 Type the error message or describe the error and click Enter on the keyboard.

5 Browse the results. If you think you've found a solution:

    a. See if you can find similar results to back up the solution.

    b. Work through the solution.

    c. Do not download anything to fix the problem for you!

 HOT TIP: If you're still getting error messages when you open a program, consider uninstalling the program and finding something newer to replace it.

! ALERT: You'll find thousands, if not hundreds of thousands, of pages on the internet that tell you that you need to download a file to fix your problem or to replace missing files, or that you need to run virus scans and run missing driver scans. Don't fall for this – it's a scam! Doing this could damage your computer with viruses, adware, spyware, or worse.

Consider an alternative program

If you've tried everything in this chapter but you still can't fix your software problems, consider an alternative program. There are lots of free programs available. In fact, Microsoft's Live Essentials suite of programs may offer everything you need. You can also get free programs from manufacturer websites. If you have a printer from Hewlett-Packard, say, visit the HP website to see what's available in the way of photo editing, for example.

1 Visit http://explore.live.com.

2 Get a Live ID.

3 Locate and click the link for Windows Live Essentials.

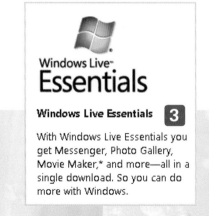

4 Read the information offered and install the programs you think you'll use.

Messenger

Stay in touch with the people you care about most from your PC, phone, or the web. Share photos and videos as you chat, and see the latest updates from your friends. Learn more

Photo Gallery

Get great tools for organizing, touching up, and sharing your photos and videos. Create stunning panoramas, movies, and slide shows, and publish them online. Learn more

Movie Maker

Turn your photos and videos into polished movies that are easy to share. Add special effects, transitions, sound, and captions to help tell your story in style. Learn more

Windows Live Mesh

Keep photos and documents in sync between your computers, and on SkyDrive. Connect remotely to all of the files and programs on your PCs. Learn more

Also included in Windows Live Essentials

Writer

Blog like a pro, adding photos, videos, maps, and more.

Family Safety

Parental controls to help parents keep their children safe online.

Mail

Manage multiple email accounts, calendars, and your contacts, even when you're offline.

Messenger Companion

See and comment on links your friends have shared as you visit websites in Internet Explorer.

Bing Bar

Get search results from Bing without leaving the website you're on.

Outlook Connector Pack

Includes Microsoft Outlook Hotmail Connector and Outlook Social Connector Provider for Messenger.

Microsoft Silverlight

Access rich, interactive websites using the Silverlight browser plug-in.

 HOT TIP: When looking for an alternative program, consider free programs from Microsoft.

 HOT TIP: Click any Live application to learn more about it.

ALERT: Beware of software that's not created by Microsoft, unless it comes from a manufacturer's website. Free software often comes with strings attached, such as adware and spyware.

Uninstall an error-prone application

If you've come this far and have found an alternative program to replace a buggy one, uninstall the buggy one to get it off your hard drive – you don't want it running in the background, trying to open when you don't want it to, or using up hard drive space.

1 Click Start, then click Control Panel.

2 Click Uninstall a program.

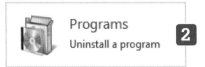

3 Locate the program in the list.

4 Click it and click Uninstall. (It may also have Change beside it.)

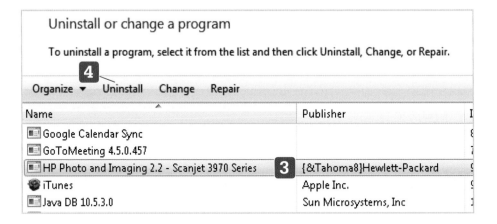

6 Repair boot problems

Introduction

When you start your computer, a few things happen in a very specific order. Among other things, the Power On Self Test (POST) occurs, program code runs and hardware is initiated, and the operating system is loaded. During this process you may see a black screen with white words, a splash screen with the computer manufacturer's name written on it, a single black, flashing cursor, a combination of these, or something else. You'll also hear at least one beep – so no, you're not hearing things!

If something goes wrong with the process and the operating system doesn't load, your computer has a 'boot' problem. You can resolve many boot problems by simply restarting the computer, believe it or not. However, that doesn't work all the time. If your computer won't boot, work through the tasks in this chapter, in order.

Restart the computer

As noted in the introduction, sometimes restarting the PC will resolve a boot-up problem. It's the equivalent of tapping the glass on a television to make a picture come on better. No one knows why, but sometimes it really works. While it's booting, listen for a single beep.

1. Before restarting the computer:
   a. Verify the keyboard is securely attached.
   b. Verify the monitor is plugged in, securely connected and powered on, if applicable.

2. Click Start and click Restart, if you can.

3. If the computer is frozen, press and hold the Power button until the computer begins to restart. Let go.

4. Watch and listen while the computer boots. You should hear only one short beep.

5. If prompted, choose Start Windows Normally.

6. If the computer boots successfully, great! If not, continue to the next section.

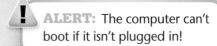

Start Windows Normally

ALERT: If you hear more than one beep, you'll probably have to take your computer to a repair shop. Multiple beeps (or a really long beep) indicate internal hardware problems, such as circuit failures or problems with RAM.

ALERT: The computer can't boot if it isn't plugged in!

Boot to the Last Known Good Configuration

Your computer saves the configuration information from the last time it was booted successfully. If you are having boot problems, you may be able to boot the computer using that configuration.

1 Use the Power button to reboot the computer.

2 As soon as you hear the boot process begin, press F8 on the keyboard repeatedly.

F8

3 Select Last Known Good Configuration.

4 If the boot process completes successfully, great! If not, continue to the next section.

Last Known Good Configuration (your most recent settings that worked)

 HOT TIP: Pressing F8 is the way to get to most of the troubleshooting options in this chapter.

 ALERT: Sometimes, the Last Known Good Configuration isn't that great. It may boot, but with errors. If the computer boots but you aren't satisfied with the results, continue troubleshooting.

 HOT TIP: If at first you don't succeed, try, try again – it may take some finesse to press F8 just at the right time.

Boot with Safe mode (and then reboot)

Safe mode offers another way to troubleshoot boot problems. As with other options, you press F8 repeatedly after the boot process begins but before the Windows 7 splash screen appears to get to it. Safe mode, if you can boot the computer into it, lets you troubleshoot in the following ways:

- See where the boot process hangs up if a complete boot cannot be achieved.
- Use Control Panel to uninstall a problematic program.
- Open Device Manager to rollback a problematic driver.
- Use System Restore to restore a previously stable computer state.

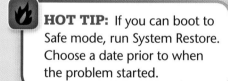 **HOT TIP:** If you can boot to Safe mode, run System Restore. Choose a date prior to when the problem started.

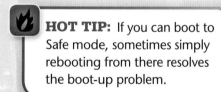 **HOT TIP:** If you can boot to Safe mode, sometimes simply rebooting from there resolves the boot-up problem.

Choose Startup Repair

If the previous tasks in this chapter haven't worked, Startup Repair just might. As with other troubleshooting options in this chapter, you have to press F8 during the boot process to access it.

1 Restart the computer and press F8 repeatedly until the Advanced Boot Options screen appears.

2 Repair Your Computer will be selected.

3 Press Enter on the keyboard.

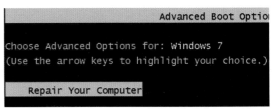

4 Select your language from the list and click Next.

5 Select your user name from the list and type your password. Click OK.

6 Click Startup Repair.

7 Click Finish. Click Restart.

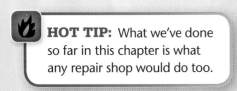

HOT TIP: What we've done so far in this chapter is what any repair shop would do too.

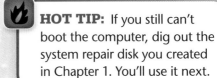

HOT TIP: If you still can't boot the computer, dig out the system repair disk you created in Chapter 1. You'll use it next.

Boot with your system repair disk

If you created a system repair disk in Chapter 1, you can try to use that now. Your computer must be able to boot from a CD/DVD though, and if yours can't you'll have to skip this step.

1 Insert the system repair disk you created in Chapter 1 into the CD/DVD drive.

2 Use the Power button to restart your computer.

3 When prompted to 'Press any key to boot from CD or DVD', press Enter on the keyboard.

4 Follow the prompts to recover your system.

```
Press any key to boot from CD or DVD...._
```

ALERT: You can configure your computer to boot to a CD or DVD from the BIOS. Messing around in there when you don't know what you're doing is risky though. If you can't boot to a CD or DVD, just skip this option.

 HOT TIP: If you've created a system image using a backup utility, you can repair your system with that image. Just click System Image Recovery when prompted.

WHAT DOES THIS MEAN?
BIOS: Stands for Basic Input/Output System. The BIOS performs tests each time you turn on your computer and then initiates the loading of the operating system.

Perform a repair installation

This is my favourite option when things go wrong: the repair installation. If you have a 'real' Windows 7 disk (not a set of recovery disks from the computer manufacturer), you can insert the disk, boot with it and repair your computer in almost all cases.

1 Insert the Windows 7 DVD.

2 Reboot the computer.

3 When prompted, press any key to boot from the CD/DVD.

4 Click Install now.

5 When prompted, choose Upgrade.

6 Complete the installation process.

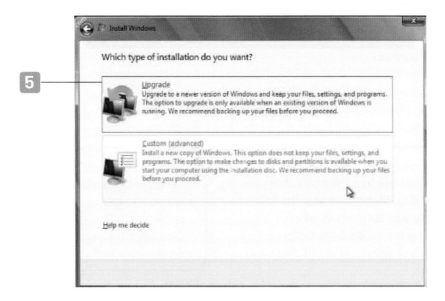

DID YOU KNOW?

When you choose to upgrade or repair Windows 7 using the Windows 7 disk, you will not lose any data, pictures, music, settings, connections or any other information.

ALERT: Recovery disks that come with many computers will reinstall the system and return it to the way it was the day you bought it. You'll lose all your data, pictures, videos, music, settings, your connection to the internet and your network, and more. We don't suggest it unless all else fails.

Run Disk Check

After you've successfully booted your computer, run Disk Check. This will help you find and repair errors on your hard drive. Problems occur when the computer tries to write to bad areas on the hard drive. To be sure that this was (or is) your problem, run a disk check.

1 Click Start and click Computer.

2 Right-click your main drive, probably C:, and click Properties.

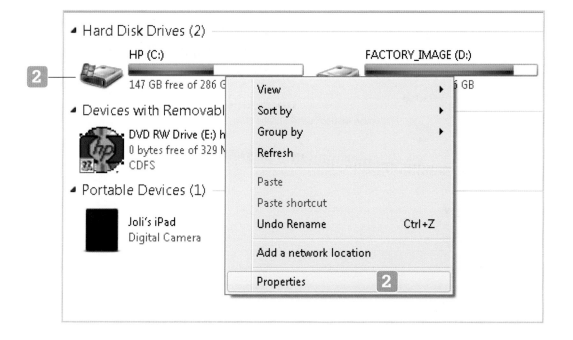

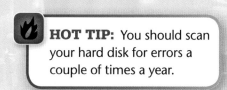 **HOT TIP:** You should scan your hard disk for errors a couple of times a year.

3 Click the Tools tab and click Check now.

4 Accept the default settings and click Start.

5 If prompted, click Schedule Disk Check.

6 Click OK.

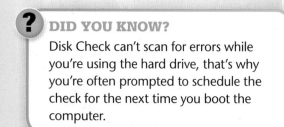

DID YOU KNOW?

Disk Check can't scan for errors while you're using the hard drive, that's why you're often prompted to schedule the check for the next time you boot the computer.

7 Diagnose and repair network problems

Introduction

Networking problems occur when you can't access the internet, can't access network devices, or both. Sometimes networking problems occur because sharing and network settings have been inadvertently changed, but most networking problems occur because something has become disconnected, has been turned off or has in some way been damaged. (If you have a puppy, it may be the result of a cable that's been used as a chew toy, for instance.) In rare instances, connection problems occur because your internet service provider (ISP) is experiencing technical difficulties. Although these problems are frustrating, if you approach the problem in the order listed here, you'll very likely be able to resolve it on your own.

Review troubleshooting tasks already introduced

You probably will not work through this book in order from start to finish. It's more likely you'll have a problem and will turn to the relevant chapter to resolve it. Thus, here's a list of things that have already been introduced and their related chapters. Do these things first!

- Reboot your cable, satellite or DSL modem, your router, and all your PCs – Chapter 2.
- Check the Action Center for problems and solutions – Chapter 2. Note you can opt to troubleshoot, shown here.
- Understand common hardware problems – Chapter 4.
- Understand common printer problems – Chapter 4.

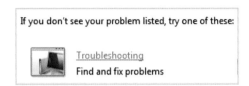

If you don't see your problem listed, try one of these:

Troubleshooting
Find and fix problems

Printer

The remaining repairs require administrator permissions

Problems found

No physical printer is installed

Hardware changes might not have been detected

 Try these repairs as an administrator

Explore additional options

View detailed information

Close

? DID YOU KNOW?
If you can connect to the internet but not a specific network device, turn that device on as well as the computer it's connected to.

🔥 HOT TIP: If you can't connect to the internet, call your internet service provider. Perhaps there's an outage in your area.

Verify required hardware is powered on

Hardware must have power and be turned on to work. If you have a penny-pinching spouse, consider that they may have powered off the hardware required to run your network before you both headed off for bed last night. If that's not the case, consider the following:

- The power cable must be securely connected to the hardware device.
- The power cable must be securely connected to a power outlet.
- If batteries are required, the battery may be depleted.
- The power cord may be damaged.
- A circuit breaker may have been overloaded and needs to be reset.
- The power outlet may be damaged.
- Windows may not recognise that the device is connected. You can use the Action Center to set what's connected.

 **ALERT:** If you run over a power cord with a desk chair on wheels, it could damage the cable so that it is no longer functional.

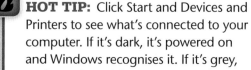 **HOT TIP:** Click Start and Devices and Printers to see what's connected to your computer. If it's dark, it's powered on and Windows recognises it. If it's grey, as shown here, it's not connected, not powered on or has some other problem.

Reconnect cables and connections

Network problems, if they aren't the result of a device (such as a modem, printer or router) being powered off, are often caused by disconnected cables or loose connections. A playful cat or grandchild can easily dislodge a connection and cables can become damaged in various ways, including being run over by a vacuum cleaner, crimped under a chair or trapped under a desk leg.

1 Inspect the cables that run from your cable modem to your computer and/or router.

2 Disconnect and reconnect every Ethernet cable.

3 Disconnect and reconnect every power cable.

4 Verify no cables are crimped or damaged.

5 Reboot your network, as outlined in Chapter 2.

6 Disconnect and reconnect other cables if you still cannot access network hardware.

? DID YOU KNOW?
Network hardware includes external hard drives, computers, laptops, scanners and anything else shared with computers on your network.

🔥 HOT TIP: Always reboot your network after powering off and on network hardware.

Reposition wireless access points

If you have grandkids, perhaps your router or wireless access point has been bumped or damaged. If the wireless router has been knocked off your desk and now sits underneath it, you could have trouble accessing the network from a laptop in the other room (or it could be so damaged it won't work and needs to be replaced).

1 Locate your wireless router and/or access points.

2 Verify there is power to the device and it is turned on.

3 Position the wireless device on a desk, towards the centre of the house.

4 From a wireless computer:
  a. Open the Network and Sharing Center (use the Start Search window to find it).
  b. Click Connect to a network.
  c. If applicable, reconnect.
  d. Click the Network icon in the taskbar to verify you're connected.

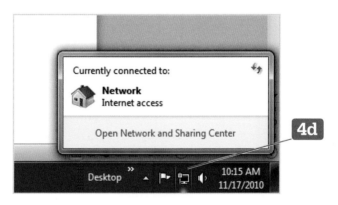

ALERT: If the network seems to be in good working order but you can't connect to it from a laptop or netbook, verify the computer's wireless networking feature is enabled (and not in Airplane mode or turned off).

HOT TIP: If, when connected via a laptop, you see only one or two bars for network signal strength, consider moving the wireless access point to a different area of the house, in a more central location.

Run the network troubleshooter

You already know that the Action Center offers troubleshooting wizards (Chapter 2) and there's one there to help you resolve networking problems. However, there's also the Network and Sharing Center. This option is easier to use than the Action Center, and you can open it right from the taskbar's Notification area.

1 Click the Network icon on the taskbar.

2 Click Open Network and Sharing Center.

3 If you see a red X, click it.

4 Follow the prompts to resolve the problem.

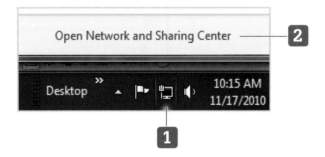

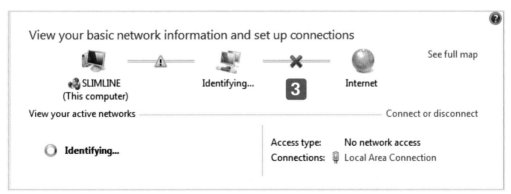

? DID YOU KNOW?

You may not see what's shown here. You may simply see your computer, an internet icon and a red X. Either way, a red X means there's a problem.

🔥 HOT TIP: You may be able to connect to resources on your local network while not being able to connect to the internet. If that's the case, call your ISP to see whether there's an outage in your neighbourhood.

Replace damaged cables, splitters and other hardware

If you've decided that you have a damaged Ethernet cable, a malfunctioning splitter, non-functional cable modem, disabled power outlet or other device, you'll have to decide whether it's something you can fix or something you need to have repaired by a professional.

- Do not attempt to repair an electrical outlet yourself, unless you're a licensed electrician.
- Do replace old, damaged or crimped Ethernet cables with new ones.
- Do troubleshoot problems by replacing old splitters or power cables.
- Do call your ISP if you think the source of your problem is a non-functional cable, satellite or DSL modem.
- Do explore other troubleshooting options, available from the Network and Sharing Center.

 HOT TIP: You may need to come back to this section after completing this chapter if you still have not found the source of your network problem. Something as small as a damaged splitter can bring down a network and the only way to find out whether that's the problem is to replace the damaged item with a new one.

WHAT DOES THIS MEAN?

Splitter: a small device that splits a signal intended for one device into a signal that can be accessed by two. Often, people split an incoming internet connection so that they can connect to both a cable modem and a TV tuner or media centre, to avoid having to 'drop' another line for the second device.

Verify your network is private

You may have a problem diametrically opposite to what's been discussed so far. It may be that your network works too well! If your neighbours can access your network, it's not locked down tightly enough. Your network should be private (set to either Home or Work, not Public). It's best to check.

1 Open the Network and Sharing Center.

2 Verify your network is set to Home (or Work).

3 If it's set to Public (not shown):

   a. Click Public to change it.

   b. Select Home, or select Work.

   c. Changes will be applied automatically.

   d. Click Close.

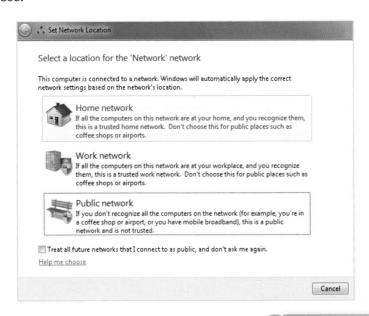

DID YOU KNOW?

Your network should be private and your router settings should be secured with a password. If you aren't sure whether your wireless network is secure, see if a guest can connect to the internet using it the next time they visit with a wireless device, such as an iPad, netbook, wireless-enabled phone or laptop.

DID YOU KNOW?

Home and Work networks are *almost* exactly the same except for their names. Learn one of the differences in the penultimate section of this chapter, 'Create a homegroup'. Ultimately, if at home, choose Home network.

Review sharing settings

You must give permission for other computers and users to view, sign in and access your network. To make the *network* available, you enable Network Discovery. To make *data* on the network accessible, you either open your network to anyone who can access the network or you limit it to those to whom you've given a user name and password, *on your computer.*

1 Open the Network and Sharing Center.

2 Click Change advanced sharing settings.

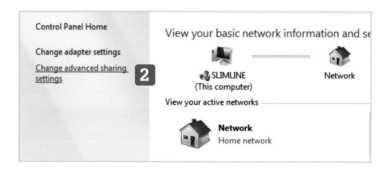

3 Your network must be visible. Verify network discovery is enabled.

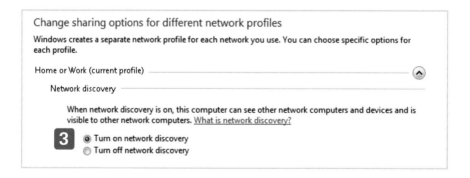

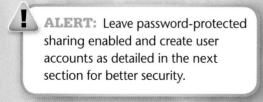

ALERT: Leave password-protected sharing enabled and create user accounts as detailed in the next section for better security.

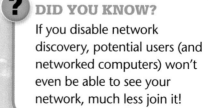

DID YOU KNOW?

If you disable network discovery, potential users (and networked computers) won't even be able to see your network, much less join it!

4 To share printers and data, file and printer sharing must be enabled and/or public sharing.

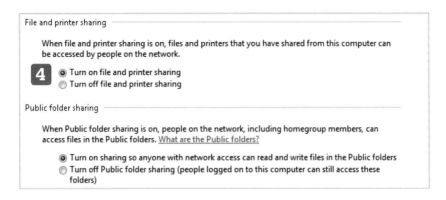

5 Explore other sharing options, specifically password-protected sharing. Consider leaving the settings as shown here.

6 Click Save changes if applicable.

HOT TIP: You should keep three security features in place: your network should be set to Home or Work; your router should be configured with a password that new users have to enter to connect to the network; and anyone connected to the network should be assigned a user name and password on your computer to access the data on it.

Create a user account

You can protect your computer from unauthorised network access by requiring potential users to enter a user name and password to access the data on it. When coupled with password-protected sharing, outlined in the previous section, you can rest assured your data is secure.

1 Click Start.

2 Click Control Panel.

3 Click Add or remove user accounts.

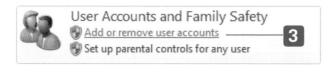

4 Click Create a new account.

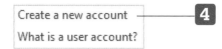

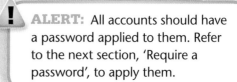

DID YOU KNOW?

You created your user account when you first turned on and set up your new Windows 7 PC. Your user account is what defines your personal folders as well as your settings for desktop background, screen saver and other items. If you share the PC with someone or allow access to it over a network, they should have their own user account.

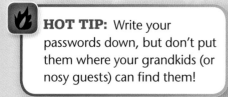

HOT TIP: Write your passwords down, but don't put them where your grandkids (or nosy guests) can find them!

ALERT: All accounts should have a password applied to them. Refer to the next section, 'Require a password', to apply them.

5 Type a new account name, verify Standard user is selected, and click Create Account.

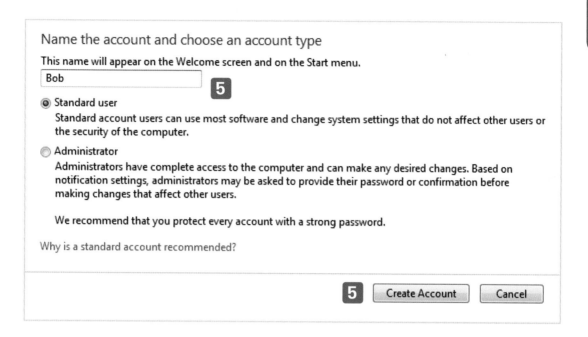

Name the account and choose an account type

This name will appear on the Welcome screen and on the Start menu.

Bob

5

⦿ Standard user

Standard account users can use most software and change system settings that do not affect other users or the security of the computer.

◯ Administrator

Administrators have complete access to the computer and can make any desired changes. Based on notification settings, administrators may be asked to provide their password or confirmation before making changes that affect other users.

We recommend that you protect every account with a strong password.

Why is a standard account recommended?

5   Create Account   Cancel

 DID YOU KNOW?

Administrators can make changes to system-wide settings but Standard users cannot (without an Administrator name and password).

HOT TIP: You can click Change the picture, Change the account name, Remove the password and other options to further personalise the account.

Require a password

All user accounts, even yours, should be password-protected. When a password is configured, you must type the password to log onto your PC or laptop. This protects the PC from unauthorised access. If password-protected sharing is enabled, users must also enter a user name and password to access your data over the network.

1 Click Start and click Control Panel.

2 Click Add or remove user accounts.

3 Click the user account you wish to apply a password to.

4 Click Create a password.

5 Type the new password, type it again to confirm it and type a password hint.

6 Click Create password.

Make changes to Bob's account

Change the account name

Create a password **4**

Change the picture

Set up Parental Controls

Bob
Standard user

! **ALERT:** If every person who accesses your PC has their own Standard user account and password, and if every person logs on using that account and then logs off the PC each time they've finished using it, you'll never have to worry about anyone accessing anyone else's personal data.

! **ALERT:** Create a password that contains upper- and lower-case letters and a few numbers. Write the password down and keep it somewhere out of sight and safe.

Remove unwanted networks

Each time you connect to a wireless network, Windows 7 remembers it and puts it in a list. When wireless capabilities are enabled, Windows 7 scans for networks to find one to connect to, starting at the top of the list. It can take a little longer to connect to a wireless network if the network you want to connect to is at the bottom. Thus, you need to occasionally remove unwanted networks and reorder what's left.

1 Open the Network and Sharing Center.

2 Click Manage wireless networks.

3 Click any network to remove.

4 Click Remove.

5 Click any network to move it up or down the list.

6 Click Move up or Move down as applicable.

Manage wireless networks **2**

Change adapter settings

Change advanced sharing settings

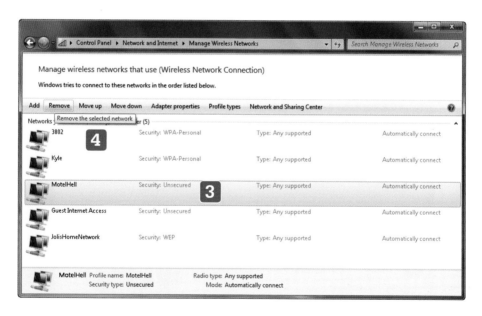

? DID YOU KNOW?
It's best to put your most used wireless networks at the top of the list and least used at the bottom.

! ALERT: You won't find the wireless network list here on a desktop computer that is not Wi-Fi enabled.

? DID YOU KNOW?
You can right-click any network to rename it, remove it or move it up or down.

Create a homegroup

If you have more than one Windows 7 computer on your home network, you can create a homegroup. Homegroups make sharing data, music, pictures, video and the like easier, because the homegroup configures the required settings for you.

1 Open the Network and Sharing Center.

2 Next to HomeGroup, click Ready to create. (A homegroup may have already been created and you may see something different.)

3 Click Create a homegroup (not shown).

4 Select what to share and click Next.

5 Write down the password so you can join the homegroup from your other Windows 7 networked PCs.

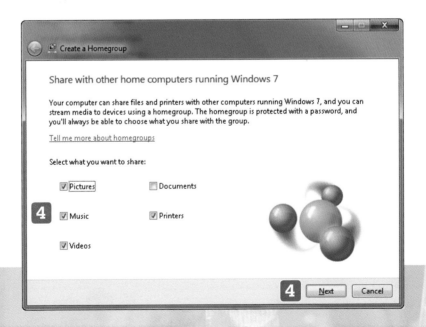

? DID YOU KNOW?
You may have created a homegroup when you set up Windows 7.

! ALERT: You can create a homegroup only if your network type is set to Home. (Work and Public won't do.)

Join a homegroup

Once you've created a homegroup on one Windows 7 computer, you can join that homegroup from any other Windows 7 computer. With your password in hand from the previous section, complete the following steps.

1 On the second Windows 7 PC, connect to the network.

2 Open the Network and Sharing Center.

3 Next to HomeGroup, click Available to join.

4 Click Join Now.

5 Click Next.

6 Type the password and click Next.

7 Click Finish.

Access type:	Internet	**3**
HomeGroup:	Available to join	
Connections:	.ılıl Wireless Network Connection (3802)	

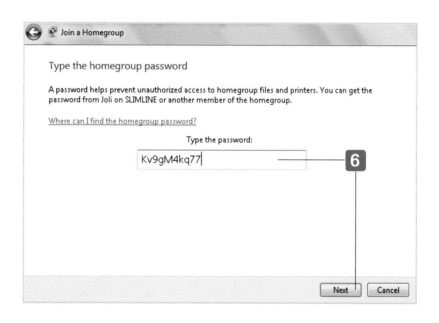

HOT TIP: If you misplaced the password between the previous section and this one, on the originating PC, open the Network and Sharing Center, click Choose homegroup and sharing options, and click View or print the homegroup password.

? DID YOU KNOW?
You can add new Windows 7 computers to your homegroup as you acquire them. In fact, you'll be offered the chance to join the homegroup during set-up, as long as Windows 7 can 'see' your network.

8 Install missing and must-have applications

Introduction

Windows 7 does not come with all you need to do everything you need to do. It does not have an email program, an instant messaging program, an image-editing program, a video messaging program or anti-virus software. It does not come with a PDF reader, a PowerPoint viewer, a way to make phone calls over the internet, a way to watch specific types of video files, or programs you may need to sync an iPod, phone or MP3 player. You have to obtain and install all of this yourself.

In this chapter you'll look at items you can get for free to round out your computing experience. Note that you may not need all of these things; if you don't want to send instant messages, there's no need to install a program to do it. However, if you want to video chat with your grandkids, send and receive email or make internet-based phone calls around the world for free, you do!

Download and installation basics

If, after reading a section in this chapter, you deem the suggested program worthy, you'll need to download and install it. For the most part, the process is the same no matter what application you choose.

1 Visit the relevant manufacturer's website.

2 Search for the product you want to download.

3 Verify you are still on the manufacturer's website and click something similar to the following:

   a. Download.

   b. Get <product name>.

   c. Download Now.

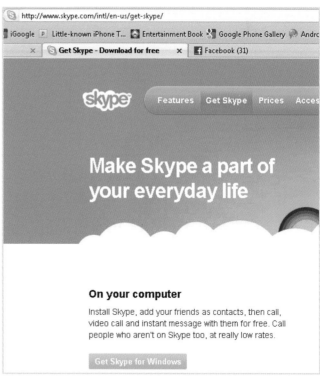

ALERT: Only install the programs listed in this chapter for now, along with any software you use to sync a phone or similar device. You can't trust everyone to write good program code, and you certainly don't want to install anything that will also place adware or spyware on your machine, hijack your web browser's home page, or otherwise cause harm.

4 Click Run. (You could click Save but you don't have to, usually.)

5 Work through the installation process.

6 Complete any remaining steps, such as getting a login ID, joining and/or signing up.

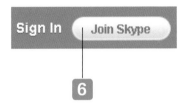

6

 HOT TIP: If you opt for Skype to communicate with others, you'll probably want to get a headphone set that includes a microphone.

ALERT: Do not download an application from a site that is *not* the manufacturer's website.

 HOT TIP: Throughout this chapter we'll be using Internet Explorer 9 to download files.

Get Windows Live Essentials

Windows Live Essentials contains all of the programs you'll need to manage email, instant message with contacts, edit photos and even create and edit your own movies. You can choose to install additional applications from the suite too, including the Internet Explorer toolbar that connects all of this seamlessly.

1. Open your web browser and navigate to http://download.live.com/.

2. Look for the Download now button and click it. You'll be prompted to click Download now once more on the next screen.

3. Click Run and when prompted, click Yes.

4. When prompted, select the items to download. You can select all of the items or just some of them. (Make sure to at least select Live Mail, Live Messenger and Live Photo Gallery.)

5. Click Install and when prompted, select the default settings.

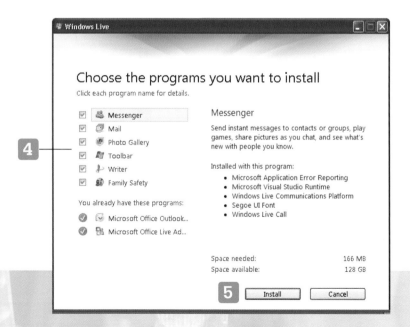

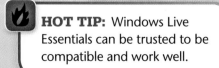

ALERT: In Chapter 9, 'Resolve email problems', we'll be discussing Windows Live Mail.

Get a Windows Live ID

When you use 'Live' services, such as Windows Live Mail, Windows Live Messenger and others, you have to log into them using a Windows Live account. This account is free and you can use it to sign into Live-related websites on the internet as well.

1 If you do not already have a Windows Live account, click Sign up after the installation of Live Mail completes. (You can also go to http://signup.live.com.)

2 Fill out the required information and click I accept when you've finished.

? DID YOU KNOW?
You can use your Windows Live email account as a regular email address, or simply use it to log into Live services on the internet.

🔥 HOT TIP: Fill out the boxes with true information. This is an ID, after all.

? DID YOU KNOW?
You'll get a free webpage you can personalise when you get a Windows Live ID.

Get Microsoft Security Essentials

Another free program available from Microsoft is Security Essentials. It's an anti-virus program. If you don't have an anti-virus program already, get this one!

1 Visit http://www.microsoft.com/security_essentials/.

2 Click Download Now.

3 Look for a dialogue box similar to this one and click Run. (You may have IE8 and we're using IE9.)

Do you want to run or save **mssefullinstall-x86fre-en-us-vista-win7.exe** (8.12 MB) from **mse.dlservice.microsoft.com**?

3 Run | Save | ▾ | Cancel

4 Work through the installation process.

5 Once installed, scan your system, get updates and perform other tasks as prompted.

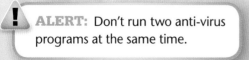

ALERT: Don't run two anti-virus programs at the same time.

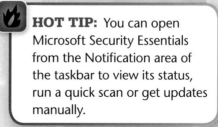

HOT TIP: You can open Microsoft Security Essentials from the Notification area of the taskbar to view its status, run a quick scan or get updates manually.

Get PowerPoint Viewer

The free PowerPoint Viewer available from Microsoft lets you view PowerPoint presentations you obtain from others. If you don't get this software and you don't have some edition of Microsoft Office (2000, 2003, 2001 or 2010) you won't be able to view them.

1 Visit www.microsoft.com/downloads.

2 Search for PowerPoint Viewer.

PowerPoint Viewer Microsoft PowerPoint Viewer lets you view full-featured presentations created in PowerPoint 97 and later versions.	5/5/2010

3 Locate PowerPoint Viewer, click it and click Download.

4 Work through the installation process.

5 Open any existing PowerPoint presentation to view it.

! ALERT: Remember, download Microsoft products from Microsoft.com only.

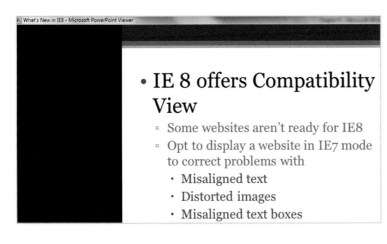

? DID YOU KNOW?

It's common to get PowerPoint presentations as email attachments with beautiful pictures of landscapes and scenery. You may even get one with pictures of your grandchild. These attachments are generally safe to view.

WHAT DOES THIS MEAN?

PowerPoint: a program in the Microsoft Office suite of applications that enables you to create and display slideshow presentations for clients, birthday parties, retirement parties and similar events.

Get Adobe Reader

Adobe Reader is an extremely popular program for viewing PDF (Portable Document Format) files. PDF files are difficult to edit by those who receive them and are thus more secure than simple text documents. You may get a PDF file in an email from a contractor that contains an estimate, from a doctor that contains lab results, or from a lawyer that contains sensitive estate information.

1 Visit http://get.adobe.com/reader/.

2 Click Download Now.

3 Click Run and work through the installation process.

4 To open Adobe Reader, double-click the link on the desktop.

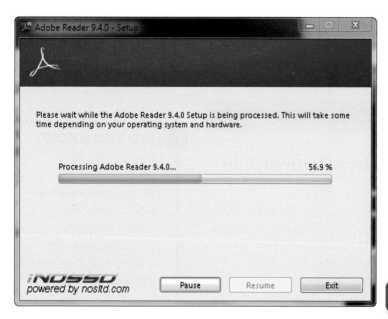

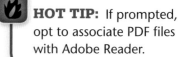
HOT TIP: If prompted, opt to associate PDF files with Adobe Reader.

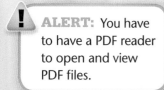
ALERT: You have to have a PDF reader to open and view PDF files.

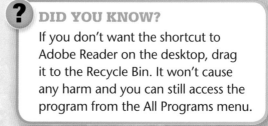
DID YOU KNOW?
If you don't want the shortcut to Adobe Reader on the desktop, drag it to the Recycle Bin. It won't cause any harm and you can still access the program from the All Programs menu.

Consider Skype™

Skype is a free program that lets you make internet-based video calls from your computer using a webcam and a headset. You can also make calls to regular phones with only a headset or a microphone and speakers. It's free to talk to other Skype users around the world. If you have children or grandchildren in other countries and it's expensive to talk to them on a regular landline or on a mobile phone, or if you'd like to see them 'in person', consider Skype.

1   Visit www.skype.com.

2   Work through the download process as detailed throughout this chapter.

3   Click Join Skype to sign up.

4   Fill out the required information.

5   Open Skype on your computer and sign in.

6   Invite others to join you on Skype and ask them to add you to their contact lists.

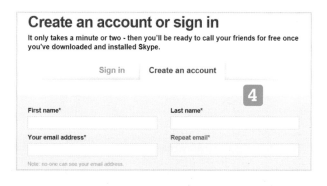

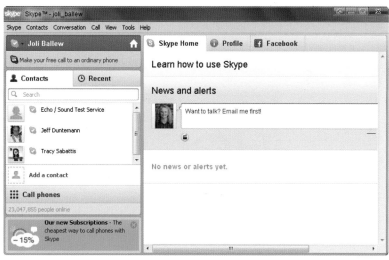

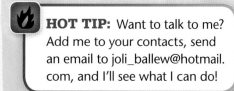

ALERT: You may be prompted to download additional items such as toolbars or search engines. Decline these.

HOT TIP: Want to talk to me? Add me to your contacts, send an email to joli_ballew@hotmail.com, and I'll see what I can do!

Consider Firefox

Firefox is a third-party web browser. Third-party web browsers get attacked by hackers less often because fewer people use them. (Hackers want to affect as many people as possible.) If you're really concerned about security, or if you simply don't like Internet Explorer, you can try Firefox.

1 Visit www.mozilla.com.

2 Download Firefox as outlined in this chapter.

3 Open Firefox.

4 Click Help to learn more.

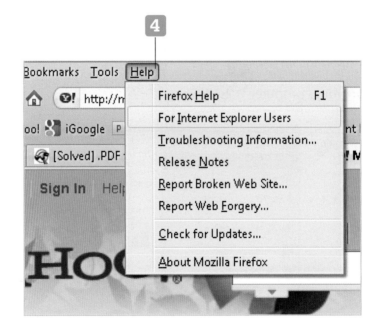

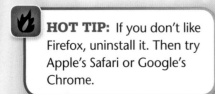

HOT TIP: If you don't like Firefox, uninstall it. Then try Apple's Safari or Google's Chrome.

ALERT: Firefox and other web browsers don't look or act like Internet Explorer. If you're not in the mood to learn another new program, stick with Internet Explorer.

9 Resolve email problems

Introduction

Windows 7 does not come with an email program. You may not need or want one though. You can use your web browser to access web-based email such as Gmail, Yahoo!, AOL and your own email provider's webpage, if you'd rather. However, we think it's best to obtain and use a computer-based email program like Windows Live Mail or Microsoft Outlook. Programs like these enable you to organise your mail in numerous ways, back up your mail and contacts easily, keep mail on your computer, and sync effectively with mobile devices, among other things.

Because there are so many email programs and web-based options available, in this chapter we'll focus on Windows Live Mail 2011. The previous chapter details how to download and install this program. We think Windows Live Mail is your best choice for many reasons: it's free, easy to use and offers lots of features.

Change how often Mail checks for email

Windows Live Mail checks for email automatically, and how often it checks depends on how you've set it up. You may want to get Mail to check for email more or less often than it does now. It's easy to make the change.

1 Open Windows Live Mail. You can find it in the All Programs menu if it isn't elsewhere.

2 Click the Menu button, click Options and click Mail.

3 Under the General tab, change the setting for Check for new messages every ... to the desired number of minutes.

4 Click OK (not shown).

HOT TIP: Drag the icon for Windows Live Mail to the taskbar and 'pin' it there.

ALERT: We're assuming you've already set up Windows Live Mail 2011 and use it as your default email program.

DID YOU KNOW?
You can change other settings in Mail from the other tabs in the Options dialogue box. Explore the tabs now.

Show images and enable links

By default, images and links are disabled in Windows Live Mail. This helps protect you in numerous ways. However, it can also hinder your ability to view, read and enjoy the email you receive, especially if it contains pictures from your children. You can enable these features in the Options window.

1 Click the Menu button and click Options.

2 Click Safety options.

3 Click the Security tab.

4 Deselect the two items related to images and external content.

5 Click OK.

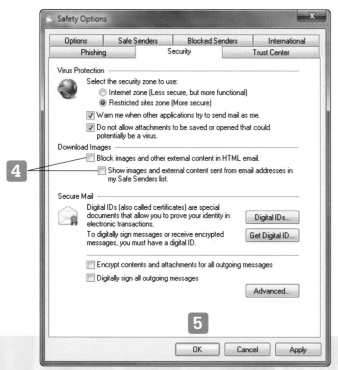

ALERT: Never click a link in an email if you do not fully trust the sender. The link could take you to a website where someone could try to steal your identity, or where spyware will be downloaded to your computer without your knowledge.

ALERT: The purpose behind disabling images automatically is two-fold. One, it prevents spammers from knowing they've reached a valid email address (there is technology that enables this in the images), and two, it takes less time to download the email when you don't also download the images.

? DID YOU KNOW?

Many of the features detailed in this chapter are also available, perhaps under different menus, in Microsoft Outlook.

Unblock attachments

Attachments are files that are 'attached' to an email and contain information that generally can't be put in the body of the email. By default, Windows Live Mail blocks you from opening potentially dangerous attachments. There are occasions where you'll need to, though, and thus have to disable this security feature.

1 Click the Menu button and click Options.

2 Click Safety Options.

3 Click the Security tab.

4 Deselect the option Do not allow attachments to be saved or opened that could potentially be a virus.

5 Click OK.

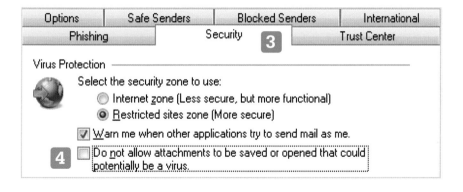

! ALERT: Never open an attachment from anyone you don't know, from a financial institution, or from an online store. Attachments can contain viruses, spyware and more.

? DID YOU KNOW? Attachments you get may contain a short video of your grandkids, an estimate for a kitchen remodel or pictures of your children.

Label email as Junk

You'll get email you don't want, from people you don't know. This is junk email, or spam. You can label a specific email as junk email to prevent receiving the same email from the same email address again.

1 Click any email that is spam.

2 Click Junk.

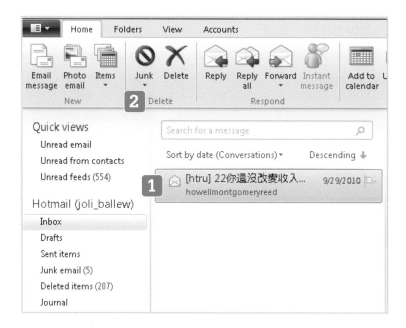

3 Click Yes to report this address to Microsoft and third parties.

4 Alternatively, click the arrow under Junk.

5 Choose the desired option from the list.

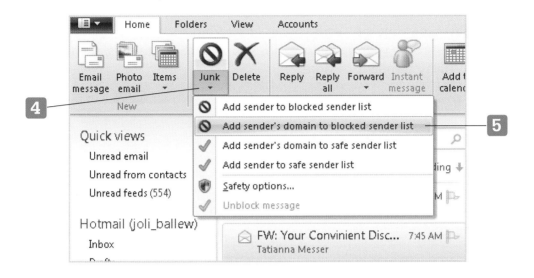

Label email as Not Junk

On occasion, an email that you want to receive will be sent to the Junk email folder. When this happens, you have to tell Windows Live Mail that it's not junk! This may happen the first time your son sends you an email from his new job, especially if he's in sales, or the first time your daughter sends you an email from hers, such as from a travel agency, utility company or store.

1 Click the Junk email folder.

2 If you see a valid email that is not junk:

   a. Click it.

   b. From the Home tab, click Not junk.

3 Alternatively, you can click the arrow under Not junk to view additional options.

4 Email declared Not junk will be sent to your Inbox.

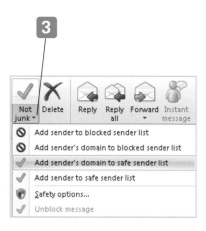

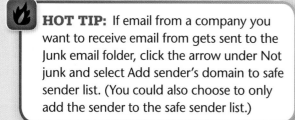

HOT TIP: If email from a company you want to receive email from gets sent to the Junk email folder, click the arrow under Not junk and select Add sender's domain to safe sender list. (You could also choose to only add the sender to the safe sender list.)

HOT TIP: Most of the information offered in this chapter can be applied to other email clients, such as Microsoft Office Outlook.

Apply a junk email filter

Most of the junk email you get will be advertisements that are scams and rip-offs, and they can also contain pornographic images. You can filter this email so you don't have to see it. There are four filtering options in Windows Live Mail: No Automatic Filtering, Low, High, and Safe List Only.

1 Click the Menus button, click Options and click Safety Options.

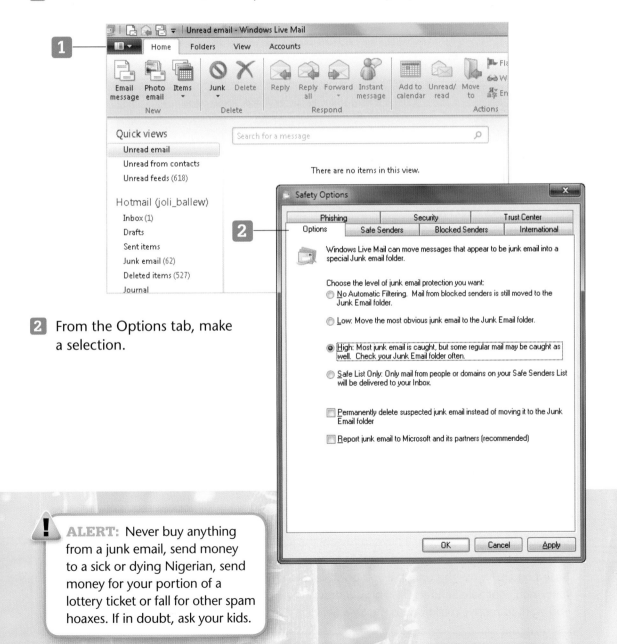

2 From the Options tab, make a selection.

> **! ALERT:** Never buy anything from a junk email, send money to a sick or dying Nigerian, send money for your portion of a lottery ticket or fall for other spam hoaxes. If in doubt, ask your kids.

3 Click the Phishing tab.

4 Select Protect my Inbox from messages with potential Phishing links. Additionally, move phishing email to the Junk email folder.

5 Click OK.

WHAT DOES THIS MEAN?

No Automatic Filtering: use this only if you do not want Windows Live Mail to block junk email messages. Windows Live Mail will continue to block messages from email addresses listed on the Blocked Senders list.

Low: use this option if you receive very little junk email. You can start here and increase the filter if it becomes necessary.

High: use this option if you receive a lot of junk email and want to block as much of it as possible. Use this option for grandchildren's email accounts. Note that some valid email will probably be blocked, so you'll have to review the junk email folder occasionally to make sure you aren't missing any email you want to keep.

Safe List Only: use this option if you only want to receive messages from people or domain names on your Safe Senders list. This is a drastic step and requires you to add every sender you want to receive mail from to the Safe Senders list. Use this as a last resort.

Empty Sent and Deleted Items folders

In order to keep Live Mail from getting bogged down, you need to delete email in folders often. Depending on how much email you get, this may be as often as once a week.

1 Right-click Junk email.

2 Click Empty 'Junk email' folder.

3 Right-click Deleted items.

4 Click Empty 'Deleted items' folder.

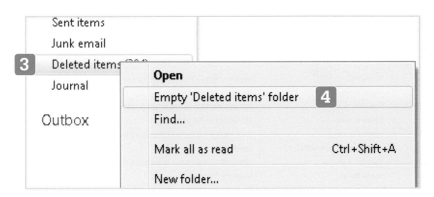

 **HOT TIP:** Select any email in any folder and click the red X to delete it.

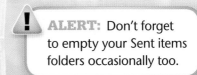 **ALERT:** Don't forget to empty your Sent items folders occasionally too.

Get rid of an email stuck in your Outbox or Inbox

On rare occasions, you'll compose an email and for whatever reason, it'll get stuck in your Outbox. A similar problem occurs when the same email arrives again and again in your Inbox. Something is hung up somewhere!

1 To resolve an Outbox problem:
  a. Click Outbox.
  b. Drag the email from the Outbox to the Inbox.
  c. Delete the email in the Inbox.

2 To resolve an Inbox problem:
  a. Visit the email provider's webpage.
  b. Log in and retrieve your email.
  c. Delete everything in the Inbox.
  d. Delete everything in the Sent and Deleted items folders.
  e. Log out and restart Live Mail.

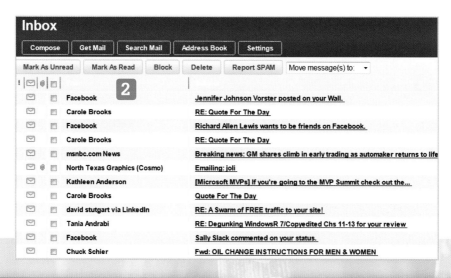

? DID YOU KNOW?

Email providers can limit how much mail you can keep and/or receive at any given time. To be safe, it's best to delete items regularly from your Inbox.

? DID YOU KNOW?

Often problems can be resolved by rebooting your computer, or even simply by closing and then reopening Live Mail. Try both.

Update the time and date on your PC

You can have problems with email if the date configured on your computer is incorrect. Check the date now in the bottom right corner and if it is not correct, change it.

1 Click the date and time in the Notification area.

2 Click Change date and time settings.

3 Click Change date and time.

4 Configure the proper date (not shown) and click OK.

5 Click OK again.

! ALERT: If, after setting your computer's clock, you notice it slows down over time, take the computer to a qualified repair technician. The battery that keeps the clock in order may need to be replaced.

! ALERT: Some secure websites rely on your computer's clock being accurate. If your clock is not accurate, you may not be able to retrieve and/or send email effectively.

Decipher error messages

You may receive error messages that say something about an incorrect or invalid POP server name, SMTP server name, or user name or password, among other things. These errors prevent you from sending or receiving email (or both). If you haven't changed anything recently, your best bet is to wait it out. Often these errors resolve themselves in a few hours (sort of like a crick in the neck!). If the problem is not resolved after a time, you'll have to take action.

1 Verify you are online by visiting a website.

2 Write down the specific error message and:

   a. Call your email provider.

   b. Follow the directions they give you to resolve the problem.

3 If your email provider can't help you:

   a. Reboot the network.
See Chapter 2.

   b. Scan with Windows Defender.
See Chapter 2.

   c. Perform a System Restore.
See Chapter 2.

   d. Perform an internet search for a solution and perform it.

   e. Delete and re-enter your email account in Live Mail (with help from your email provider).

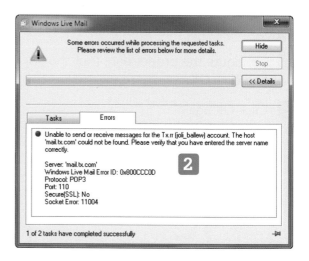

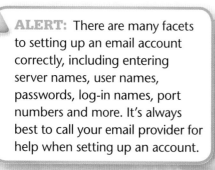

> **ALERT:** There are many facets to setting up an email account correctly, including entering server names, user names, passwords, log-in names, port numbers and more. It's always best to call your email provider for help when setting up an account.

Export contacts

You may want to export your contacts so that you can use them on another computer. You may export them so that you can then import them into a spreadsheet or database. Of course, you may simply want to back up your contacts for safe keeping. Whatever the case, Windows Live Mail makes it easy.

1 Click Contacts.

2 Click the arrow under Export.

3 Click Comma separated values.

4 Click Browse.

5 Select a location to save the contacts.

6 Type a name for the file (such as Contacts) and click Save.

7 Click Next.

8 Select the desired fields. Be sure to select at least name and email address.

9 Click Finish.

10 At the bottom of the Live Mail interface, click the Mail icon to return to your Inbox.

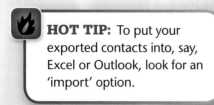

HOT TIP: To put your exported contacts into, say, Excel or Outlook, look for an 'import' option.

DID YOU KNOW?

You can export your email messages, too. Just click the Menus button, click Export Email and click Email Messages.

10 Resolve problems with Internet Explorer 8

Introduction

You might use Internet Explorer as your web browser, or you might see something else like Safari or Google Chrome. However, Internet Explorer is the most popular of all web browsers, so we've dedicated a chapter to it here. If you use another web browser, you can still apply most of what's here, although the process will be a little different.

The problems you'll encounter most with Internet Explorer 8 (IE8) aren't going to be issues with the software itself. Most of the time, problems will stem from a failed internet connection, third-party add-ons, or from websites that have yet to become IE8 compliant. However, it is certainly possible for other things to go awry in other ways, no matter how obscure. In this chapter we'll look at the common and the not-so-common issues.

Rule out network problems

Before you go any further into this chapter, make sure you're online and that your network is functional. You can't access any websites unless you can connect to the internet. There are lots of ways to uncover network issues.

- Visit the Network and Sharing Center. You'll see a red X if you aren't connected to the internet. The network shown here is healthy.

- Check the status lights on your internet modem and/or router. You should see an 'online' light and it should be lit.

- Send an email with Windows Live Mail or another computer-based program. Look for errors.

SEE ALSO: If you find that you are not connected to the internet, refer to Chapter 7 to resolve the issue.

HOT TIP: If you're using a wireless connection, check the number of bars you have. If you have only one or two bars, you may not be able to connect to the internet until you move closer to the wireless access point.

HOT TIP: If you click the red X in the Network and Sharing Center, diagnostics included with Windows 7 will run and may well offer up a reason for your connection issues.

Use Compatibility View

When IE8 was released, not all websites were ready. Websites that aren't up to the task may look 'funny' when you view them. Perhaps the images don't line up correctly, the fonts look weird, or links that should be available are nowhere to be found. You can resolve these problems by showing the site in Compatibility View.

1 In IE8, navigate to any webpage.

2 If the webpage does not appear as you believe it should, click the Compatibility View button.

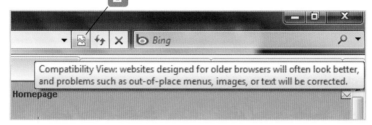

3 If prompted to set up Compatibility View, choose Express.

4 If applicable, click Tools, then click Compatibility View Settings.

5 Review the available settings.

6 Click Close.

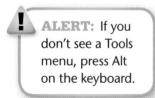

ALERT: If you don't see a Tools menu, press Alt on the keyboard.

? DID YOU KNOW?
Compatibility View shows the website in an earlier IE environment.

! ALERT: You may not see the Compatibility View button. Refer to 'Show toolbars' later in this chapter if you can't see it. Also note that not all websites offer this button, such as www. microsoft.com; it's already compatible.

Change security settings

You may experience problems if your security settings are too high. Extremely high security settings may disable features you need to view a website properly. If opting for Compatibility View doesn't work, check your security settings.

1 Press Alt on the keyboard if you can't see the Tools menu.

2 Click Tools and click Internet Options.

3 Click the Security tab.

4 If security is set to High, move the slider down to Medium-high. (If it's on Medium-high, slide down to Medium.)

5 Click OK.

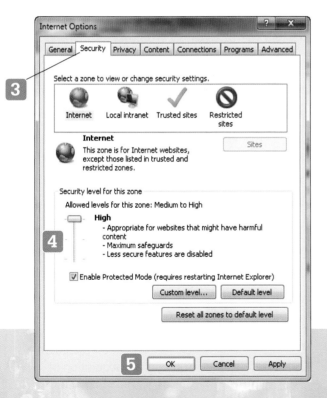

ALERT: Although you'd think that the highest security settings would be best, if you couple a lower setting with anti-virus and anti-malware/spyware software, and you stay away from pornographic sites, file-sharing sites and the like, you should be okay with a lower setting.

HOT TIP: Click the Tools menu again (step 2) and explore the other options, such as Reopen Last Browsing Session and Windows Update.

Verify cookies are enabled

Cookies are small text files that websites place on your hard drive to enhance your web surfing experience. It's what enables, say, Amazon.com, to greet you with 'Hello, Bob!'. Some websites require cookies to be enabled for them to work properly. If you're still having trouble viewing a particular website, verify that cookies are enabled.

1 Press Alt on the keyboard if you can't see the Tools menu.

2 Click Tools and click Internet Options.

3 Click the Privacy tab.

4 Click Advanced.

5 If applicable, deselect Override automatic cookie handling.

6 Click OK and OK.

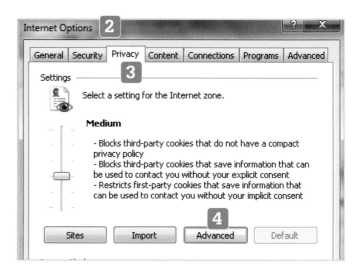

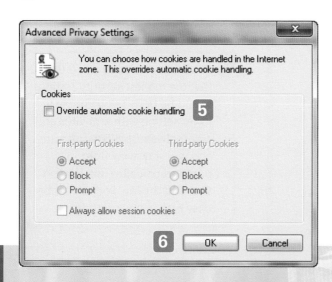

🔥 HOT TIP: If you don't want to leave any trace of what you've been looking at on the internet, including the acquisition of cookies, start an InPrivate browsing session from the Tools menu. You may want to do this when shopping for presents, for instance.

Manage add-ons

If you can view webpages but the entire surfing experience seems to have slowed down over time, it may be because of add-ons you've acquired. These come in the form of toolbars, 'link helpers', 'sign-in helpers', plug-ins and more. The more you have, the slower browsing will be.

1 Click Tools and click Manage Add-ons.

2 In the Show drop-down list, choose All add-ons.

3 Verify Add-on Types is set to Toolbars and Extensions.

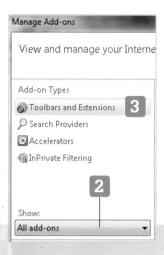

ALERT: Sometimes you inadvertently acquire a toolbar or plug-in when you download and install an application. Skype, for instance, adds a plug-in, as do other web-based applications including Windows Live.

ALERT: Don't disable any add-ons you don't recognise without doing some research. You need quite a few of these, including Microsoft Silverlight, Windows Live Mail, Shockwave Flash Object and others.

4 Browse through the add-ons, looking for items you recognise but don't use.

5 If you see a plug-in or add-on you don't use, and you see the Disable option, click it.

6 Click Disable again to verify.

7 Repeat as necessary, then click Close.

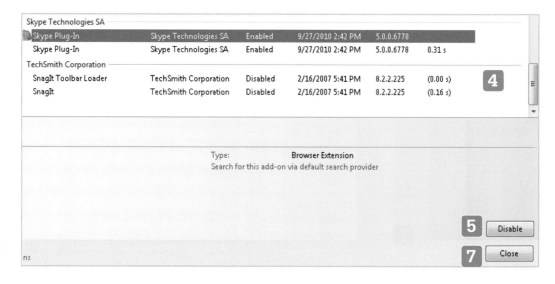

Skype Technologies SA					
Skype Plug-In	Skype Technologies SA	Enabled	9/27/2010 2:42 PM	5.0.0.6778	
Skype Plug-In	Skype Technologies SA	Enabled	9/27/2010 2:42 PM	5.0.0.6778	0.31 s
TechSmith Corporation					
SnagIt Toolbar Loader	TechSmith Corporation	Disabled	2/16/2007 5:41 PM	8.2.2.225	(0.00 s)
SnagIt	TechSmith Corporation	Disabled	2/16/2007 5:41 PM	8.2.2.225	(0.16 s)

Type: Browser Extension
Search for this add-on via default search provider

5 Disable

7 Close

ns

 DID YOU KNOW?
You can always disable an add-on now and enable it later when you need it.

 HOT TIP: In the left pane of the Manage Add-ons window, click Search Providers and Accelerators to see what's offered there. Click any item in the right pane to manage it.

Reset Internet Explorer settings

If you've made a lot of changes to Internet Explorer and you're afraid your changes have caused more problems than were there to begin with, you can reset IE8 to its default settings. This may also be your only option if you've yet to find the solution to the particular problem you're having.

1 Click Tools, then click Internet Options.

2 Click the Advanced tab.

3 Click Reset.

4 Click OK.

5 Read the information offered and click OK.

6 Click OK again to close the Internet Options dialogue box.

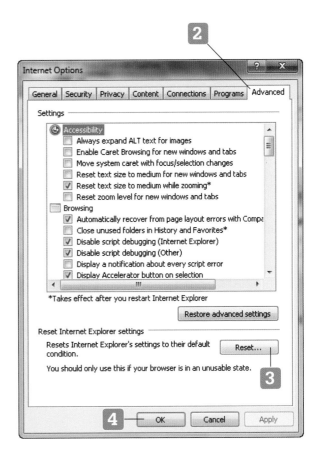

DID YOU KNOW?
When you reset IE8 you disable toolbars and add-ons, tabbed browsing settings and pop-up settings, among other things.

Run the Malicious Software Removal Tool

The problems you are having with IE8 could be the result of 'malicious software' such as worms and similar threats. Microsoft releases an update to the Malicious Software Removal Tool on the first Tuesday of each month to help keep up with these. If you think you've been infected, you can run it to find out.

1 Visit http://www.microsoft.com/security/malwareremove/default.aspx.

2 Click Skip the details and download the tool.

3 Click Download and click Run.

4 Click Next and click Quick scan.

5 Click Next.

6 Click View detailed results of the scan.

7 Click OK and Finish.

8 Review the results and take any necessary action.

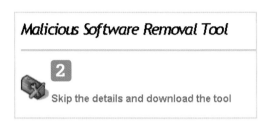

Malicious Software Removal Tool

2

Skip the details and download the tool

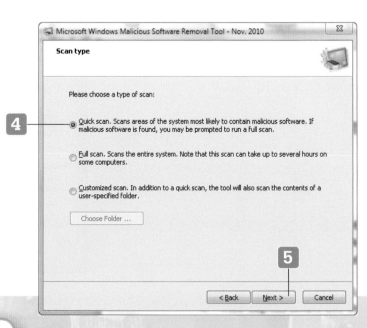

Microsoft Windows Malicious Software Removal Tool - Nov. 2010

Scan type

Please choose a type of scan:

4

○ Quick scan. Scans areas of the system most likely to contain malicious software. If malicious software is found, you may be prompted to run a full scan.

○ Full scan. Scans the entire system. Note that this scan can take up to several hours on some computers.

○ Customized scan. In addition to a quick scan, the tool will also scan the contents of a user-specified folder.

Choose Folder ...

5

< Back | Next > | Cancel

HOT TIP: If you need anti-virus software but can't afford it, try Microsoft Security Essentials. Make sure you download it from Microsoft's website and no other.

ALERT: The Malicious Software Removal Tool is not a substitute for obtaining and installing anti-virus software.

Get online support

There's quite a bit of online support available if you still haven't been able to resolve the problems you're having with IE8.

1 Click Help and click Online Support.

2 Browse the options on the page to locate a solution.

3 Look for Top Issues – you may find the solution you're looking for there.

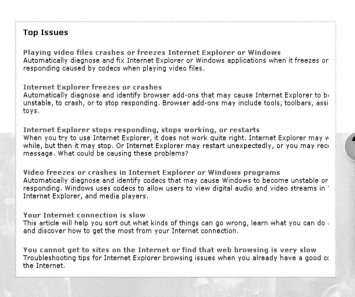

? DID YOU KNOW?

Look for a 'Microsoft Fix It' option when browsing online support. Fix It options are completed for you and are automated. No muss, no fuss!

Check for an update

When we wrote this book, IE8 was the most up-to-date browser. However, at that time, IE9 was in Beta, meaning it was to be released soon. If you're still having problems and you're up for a change, consider upgrading to IE9 now.

1 Visit www.microsoft.com/windows/internet-explorer.

2 Look for Internet Explorer 9.

3 Click Upgrade now.

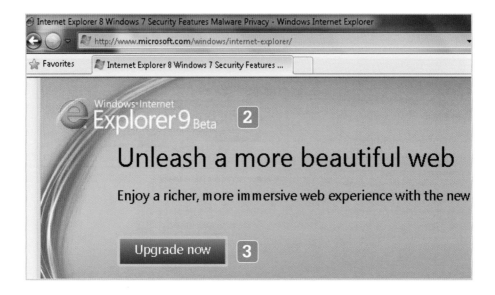

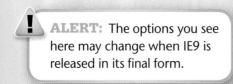

ALERT: The options you see here may change when IE9 is released in its final form.

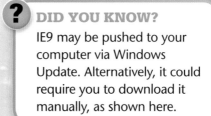

DID YOU KNOW?
IE9 may be pushed to your computer via Windows Update. Alternatively, it could require you to download it manually, as shown here.

Show toolbars

Sometimes the problem isn't that you can't access a website but that you are simply tired of pressing the Alt key to view the toolbar you need to access. Perhaps you want to see even more toolbars, including those that come with add-ons, the Command bar or the Status bar.

1 Right-click the empty area to the right of an open tab.

2 Select any toolbar you'd like to open.

3 Note the new toolbars near the tabs.

HOT TIP: To remove any toolbar, right-click again and remove the tick mark beside the toolbar by clicking it once.

WHAT DOES THIS MEAN?

Menu bar: the toolbar we've been using in this chapter that contains File, Edit, View, Favorites, Tools and Help.

Favorites bar: the toolbar that contains a quick link to your favourite websites.

Command bar: the toolbar that contains icons for Home, RSS, Mail, Print, Page, Safety, Tools, Help and more.

Status bar: the bar that runs across the bottom of the screen that shows the status of your current web activity.

Delete unwanted Favorites

Favorites are websites you add (from the Favorites menu) so that you can easily access them later. If your list gets too long, it will be hard to find what you want. You can easily delete items you no longer need.

1 Click Favorites.

2 Right-click any Favorite to delete.

3 Click Delete.

4 Right-click any Favorite listed on the Favorites bar (if that bar is showing).

5 Click Delete to remove it.

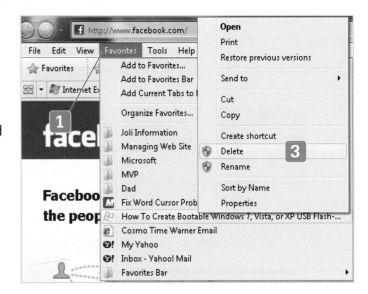

? DID YOU KNOW?
You can rename Favorites by right-clicking as well.

🔥 HOT TIP: Click Organize Favorites to create folders and move your current Favorites into them.

11 Resolve security warning messages

Introduction

You'll get security messages on your computer, especially the first few months you use it. Microsoft and Windows 7 want you to know if your computer or your data are in danger of being compromised. You'll also see messages if you are trying to view a website that's been reported as unsafe, or if you're trying to open an email that contains a potentially dangerous attachment. All of this is not meant to annoy you, it's meant to keep you safe.

Know the difference between system and third-party messages

When *any* message appears in the bottom right corner of your screen, read it but don't click it. It may not be from Windows 7. It may be a virus, adware, spyware, or it may be a message from printer or scanner software, a third-party program or a third-party website. You can check for valid Windows 7 messages in the Action Center.

1 When you see a message appear on your computer, read it.

ALERT: When you see security messages, check the Action Center to see what's going on. Don't click the message.

2 Write down the program name and/or message.

3 Open the Action Center. If you see the same message there, it's a valid message from Windows 7.

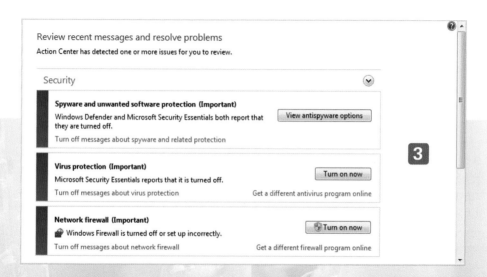

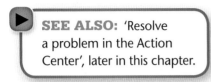

4 If you do not see the same message in the Action Center, it is one of the following:

    a. A valid message from a third-party program such as Adobe Reader.

    b. A valid message from a printer or scanner informing you of a software update.

    c. A valid message from third-party software you've installed.

    d. A virus, worm or other threat.

5 Research the message. If you feel the message is a threat:

    a. Run a virus scan using your anti-virus software. (Enable the software if necessary.)

    b. If no software exists, run Windows Defender.

    c. If no threat is found, run the Malicious Software Removal Tool (Chapter 10).

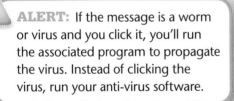

▶ **SEE ALSO:** 'Resolve a problem in the Action Center', later in this chapter.

! **ALERT:** If the message is a worm or virus and you click it, you'll run the associated program to propagate the virus. Instead of clicking the virus, run your anti-virus software.

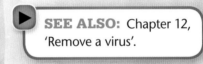

▶ **SEE ALSO:** Chapter 12, 'Remove a virus'.

Explore the Action Center

The Action Center offers information about warnings that appear as a pop-up in the bottom right corner of your screen. It's always safer to open the Action Center to resolve these warnings than to risk clicking a pop-up that isn't from Windows 7.

1 In the Notification area, click the icon that looks like a flag. It might have a red X on it.

2 Click Open Action Center.

3 Maximise the Action Center window.

4 Read all of the information offered.

5 Continue to the next section to resolve the issues.

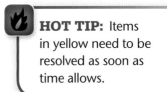

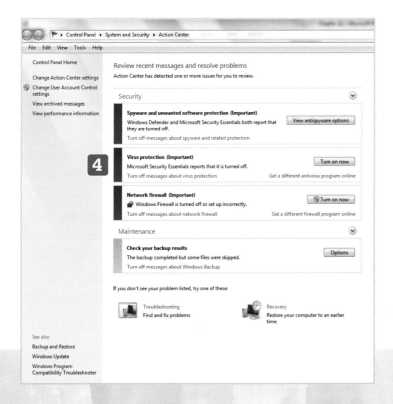

> 🔥 **HOT TIP:** Items in red need to be resolved immediately.

> 🔥 **HOT TIP:** Items in yellow need to be resolved as soon as time allows.

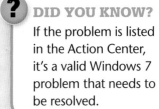

> ❓ **DID YOU KNOW?**
> If the problem is listed in the Action Center, it's a valid Windows 7 problem that needs to be resolved.

Resolve a problem in the Action Center

When there's a security problem in the Action Center, there's always an option to resolve it. Some resolutions are easy, for instance turning on the firewall. Others take more time, such as shopping for anti-virus software.

1 Open the Action Center.

2 Select a problem to resolve.

3 Click the solution offered. (Here, that's Turn on now.)

4 If prompted, verify you want to perform the solution.

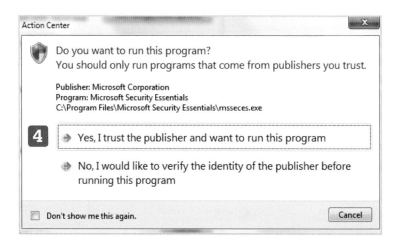

5 In some instances, you may opt to turn off specific messages.

6 Repeat until all problems are resolved.

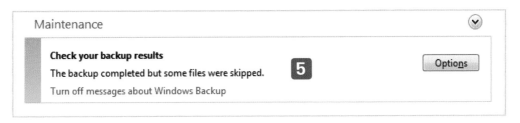

 HOT TIP: Check the Action Center once a week to see if any solutions to problems you've encountered are now available.

 HOT TIP: We think it's best to leave all messages enabled. In some instances though, such as when you have a backup plan that does not include Windows Backup and Restore, you can disable the messages.

 DID YOU KNOW?
When the Action Center has found problems, there will be a red X over the flag icon in the Notification area.

Uninstall unwanted manufacturer update software

Some software you install will prompt you to update the software regularly. Sometimes, the 'updating' software is separate from the original software. You can uninstall this software in the Control Panel. Additionally, you can disable updates from inside a program.

1 Open Control Panel.

2 Click Uninstall a program.

3 If you see update software for a program you rarely use, you can opt to uninstall it.

Apple Application Support
Apple Mobile Device Support
Apple Software Update
Audible Download Manager
AudibleManager
Bing Bar

4 You can also disable updates inside programs:

  a. Open any program for which you get update messages.

  b. Look through the menus for Preferences or Options settings.

  c. Opt out of automatic updates.

Check for updates

Adobe recommends that you automatically install updates.

○ Automatically install updates

○ Automatically download updates, but let me choose when to install them

◉ Do not download or install updates automatically

ALERT: Most updates are necessary to keep the software safe and secure, but other updates simply enhance features. We think if you use the program regularly, you should get the updates too.

HOT TIP: If you don't want the updates, perhaps you don't need the program either. Uninstall programs you no longer use for best performance and fewer pop-ups and interruptions.

Check the security report for a website

You can use Internet Explorer 8 to check for security issues with a website you're visiting. If you're ever in doubt, it's a nice safeguard to have.

1 In Internet Explorer 8, visit any website.

2 Click Safety.

3 Click Security report.

4 Read the information and click Should I trust this site?

5 Read the information offered.

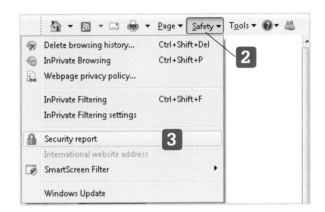

? DID YOU KNOW?
If you navigate to a website that's been reported as dangerous by users who've previously accessed it, a warning will appear. You will be encouraged not to enter the site.

HOT TIP: The Safety icon is on the Command bar. If you can't see it, refer to Chapter 10 in the section 'Show toolbars', to add it.

View all parts of an email

Sometimes email will arrive and you'll be unable to view all of its parts. Perhaps you can't click links, can't view embedded pictures or can't open attachments. This is to keep you safe. However, if you know the email is from someone you trust, you can override these default settings.

1 In any email program, click an email that offers a limited view.

2 If an option appears at the top of the page to Show images, click it.

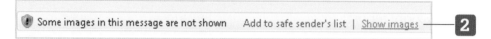

3 You may also be able to left-click or right-click the email message to explore other options.

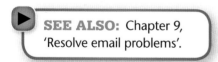

SEE ALSO: Chapter 9, 'Resolve email problems'.

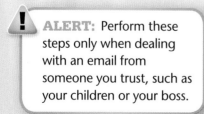

ALERT: Perform these steps only when dealing with an email from someone you trust, such as your children or your boss.

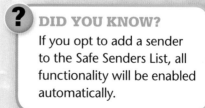

DID YOU KNOW?

If you opt to add a sender to the Safe Senders List, all functionality will be enabled automatically.

Turn off security messages

We don't suggest it, but it is possible to turn off security messages generated by the Action Center. Unfortunately, reducing the messages you see can make your computer and your data vulnerable to computer hackers. However, if specific messages are bothering you, it is possible to disable them.

1 Open the Action Center.

2 Click Change Action Center settings.

3 Deselect the items for which you no longer want to receive messages.

4 Click OK.

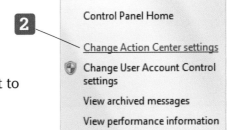

Control Panel Home

Change Action Center settings

Change User Account Control settings

View archived messages

View performance information

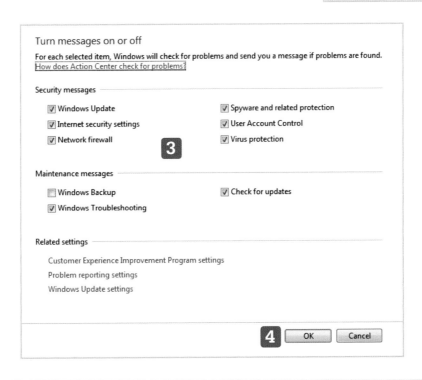

Turn messages on or off

For each selected item, Windows will check for problems and send you a message if problems are found. How does Action Center check for problems?

Security messages

- ☑ Windows Update
- ☑ Internet security settings
- ☑ Network firewall
- ☑ Spyware and related protection
- ☑ User Account Control
- ☑ Virus protection

Maintenance messages

- ☐ Windows Backup
- ☑ Windows Troubleshooting
- ☑ Check for updates

Related settings

Customer Experience Improvement Program settings

Problem reporting settings

Windows Update settings

OK   Cancel

ALERT: It's okay to disable backup messages from Backup and Restore if you have another backup plan in place.

DID YOU KNOW?

The Action Center won't recognise every anti-virus program you can potentially install and may still send security messages even though you're protected. This is another valid reason for disabling specific security messages.

12 Remove a virus

Introduction

A computer virus is like a human virus. It's passed from one computer to another. Sometimes a virus is passed via email, other times it's obtained from a website or web link. You may get a virus when you download unsafe software, click a link on a webpage, or even when you're just innocently surfing the web. We're hoping against hope you have some sort of anti-virus software installed. This will make the task of getting rid of the virus easier. If you don't have this software there are options, but it may require you to take your computer to a technician or repair shop, or worse, format and reinstall your computer from scratch.

Know the signs of a virus

You should suspect your computer has a virus if it starts doing things it should not. It may send out emails to everyone in your address book, fill your screen with pop-up advertisements, or allow you to navigate to only one webpage (often to purchase something that will magically 'cure' the problem you're having). Here are some other things you may encounter:

- Your desktop background picture has changed.
- Icons have been moved or are not available.
- The computer runs extremely slowly.
- You get error messages telling you to 'click here' to resolve problems and they aren't coming from your anti-virus program.
- The hard drive is making noises because it's overworked.
- Your anti-virus program informs you it's found a threat.

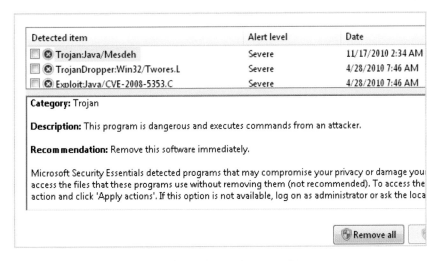

ALERT: If you can visit only a single webpage and nothing else, you've probably found the cause of the virus, or are well on your way to discovering it.

? DID YOU KNOW?
Viruses can attach themselves to parts of a website, such as a tab or link, and the website owner won't know anything about it until people start complaining. Always keep updated anti-virus software running in the background.

 HOT TIP: Most experts agree that you should disable System Restore if you think you have a virus.

First steps

If you suspect a virus you should take some immediate precautions to prevent spreading it and to minimise damage. First, close any open email program, and second, disconnect from your home network. These steps will prevent you from spreading the virus. Here are a few other things you can do:

- Disable System Restore. See Chapter 2.
- Disconnect external backup drives as a precaution.
- Close all programs. Use the Task Manager if you have to.
- Back up documents, pictures, music and other data.
- Store the backups on a flash drive or external hard drive, away from existing backups.

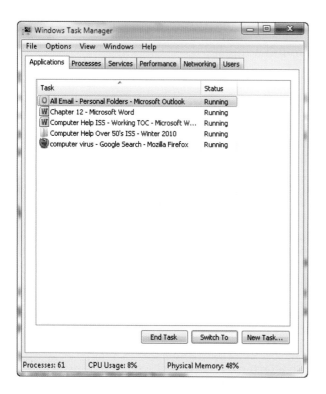

ALERT: Your personal data may be affected, but back it up anyway. In a worst-case scenario, a technician may be able to salvage the data for you.

WHAT DOES THIS MEAN?

Task Manager: you open the Task Manager by pressing Ctrl+Alt+Del. Use the Task Manager to close open programs if they won't close on their own. You may be able to close some of the virus pop-up messages as well.

Install anti-virus updates

If you have anti-virus software, get the latest updates (also called definitions). You can do that from inside the anti-virus program. There's a good chance you can't open that program; the virus may have disabled it. However, it's worth a shot.

1 Connect to the internet.

2 Locate and open your anti-virus software program – it may be in the taskbar's Notification area.

3 Look for an option to update the protection definitions:

   a. In Microsoft Security Essentials, click the Update tab and click Update.

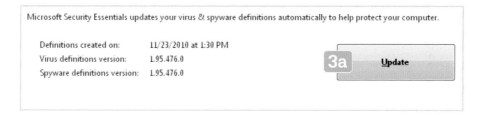

   b. In Windows Defender, from Home, click Check for updates now.

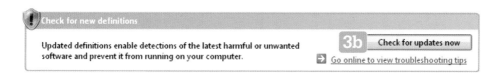

   c. Perform similar steps in other programs.

4 Disconnect from the internet when you've finished.

WHAT DOES THIS MEAN?
Definitions: files your anti-virus software maker creates to locate and destroy unwanted software, such as viruses and spyware.

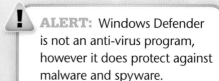 **ALERT:** Windows Defender is not an anti-virus program, however it does protect against malware and spyware.

Run anti-virus software scans

Once you've obtained the latest definitions for your anti-virus program, you can scan the computer for a virus. If your anti-virus software finds a virus and recognises it, it may be able to remove (or quarantine) the malicious files.

1 Open your anti-virus software.

2 Look for an option to scan for viruses, malware and/or spyware.

3 Click the option to scan the computer.

4 If you don't have any anti-virus software, scan with Windows Defender.

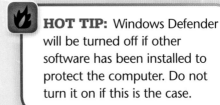

ALERT: You may not be able to run an anti-virus scan. In this instance you'll probably have to perform the removal steps manually.

HOT TIP: Windows Defender will be turned off if other software has been installed to protect the computer. Do not turn it on if this is the case.

Choose an online solution

If you don't have anti-virus software, you can try purchasing it and installing it, then running it to see if the problem can be resolved. Unfortunately, some viruses prevent you from getting online and/or accessing the option to install software, and since we've already suggested you disconnect from the internet, you're not even online to try. However, this may be your only option.

1　Reconnect to the internet if you can.

2　Visit a reputable website, such as Symantec, STOPzilla or AVG.

3　Download and install anti-virus software.

4　Get the latest updates, if possible.

5　If applicable, locate the option to scan your computer or solve a specific problem.

Anti-Spyware Made Easy!™

✓ Detects, blocks, and quarantines Spyware and Adware in true real time.
✓ Four configurable types of on-demand and automatic Spyware scanning.
✓ Can be set to update automatically or on demand for optimal protection.
✓ Advanced Pop-up protection blocks ads that slow down your surfing.
✓ Kills browser hijackers, removes rootkits, prevents botnet attacks.
✓ Blocks Phishing attacks, protects from malicious Web sites.

CLICK HERE TO DOWNLOAD STOPzilla NOW! ❯❯
Compatible with Windows 7, Vista, 2000 and XP

3

HOT TIP: If you can't get online to download a program, download it using another computer, burn it to a CD and try to install the software from the CD at the infected computer.

ALERT: Lots of 'anti-virus' software and associated scanners are actually viruses themselves. Download and install software from reputable sites only.

HOT TIP: If you can't get online, you may be able to reboot in Safe mode with Networking (F8 during boot-up) and get online that way.

Use the Malicious Software Removal Tool

If you can't get online and you can't install anti-virus software and get the newest definitions, *and* if you've been following this book from the beginning, you just may have the Malicious Software Removal Tool on your computer. You can run it to check for malicious software.

1 Open the Malicious Software Removal Tool.

2 Click Next to start the scan.

3 Click Full Scan and click Next (not shown).

4 Perform whatever steps are necessary to remove detected viruses, spyware and other threats.

SEE ALSO: Chapter 10, 'Run the Malicious Software Removal Tool'.

? DID YOU KNOW?

The Malicious Software Removal Tool is free and it's from Microsoft. It's safe.

Look on the internet for removal instructions

Your previous attempts to rid the computer of the virus may have merely provided you with its name but no resolution. The name may be all you need though – you just might find removal instructions on the internet.

1 From another computer, search for <virus name> 'removal instructions'.

2 Search until you locate step-by-step directions.

3 Print the instructions.

4 Perform the steps on the infected computer.

5 If the steps seem too complicated or risky, take the computer to a qualified technician.

---

4. To delete the value from the registry
Important: Symantec strongly recommends that you back up the registry before making any changes to it. Incorrect changes to the registry can result in permanent data loss or corrupted files. Modify the specified subkeys only. For instructions refer to the document: How to make a backup of the Windows registry.
1. Click **Start > Run**.
2. Type **regedit**
3. Click OK.

   Note: If the registry editor fails to open the threat may have modified the registry to prevent access to the registry editor. Security Response has developed a tool to resolve this problem. Download and run this tool, and then continue with the removal.

4. Navigate to and delete the following registry entries:

   - HKEY_CURRENT_USER\Software\HP35
   - HKEY_LOCAL_MACHINE\Software\HP35
   - HKEY_LOCAL_MACHINE\SYSTEM\CurrentControlSet\Services\SKYNET[EIGHT RANDOM CHARACTERS]
   - HKEY_CURRENT_USER\Software\Microsoft\Windows\CurrentVersion\FXS
   - HKEY_CURRENT_USER\Software\Microsoft\Windows\CurrentVersion\solashit2
   - HKEY_CURRENT_USER\Software\Microsoft\Windows\CurrentVersion\sunshit2
   - HKEY_LOCAL_MACHINE\Software\Microsoft\Windows\CurrentVersion\Explorer\JQS16
   - HKEY_CURRENT_USER\Software\Microsoft\Windows\CurrentVersion\Explorer\Wallpaper\XMAS
   - HKEY_CURRENT_USER\Software\Microsoft\Installer
   - HKEY_CURRENT_USER\SOFTWARE\Microsoft\instkey
   - HKEY_CURRENT_USER\SOFTWARE\Microsoft\cavok
   - HKEY_LOCAL_MACHINE\SOFTWARE\Microsoft\Windows\CurrentVersion\Control
   - Panel\Settings\"Time"
   - HKEY_LOCAL_MACHINE\SOFTWARE\Microsoft\Windows\CurrentVersion\Run\"Wind River Systems" =

 ALERT: While searching for ways to remove the virus you'll run across plenty of utilities that claim they can do it for you, for a price. Most of the time this is a scam or will worsen the problem by complicating it with spyware and malware.

 HOT TIP: Although most virus-removal websites are scams, there are some that are not. AVG, Symantec, PCTools and STOPzilla are OK.

Final steps

If you think you've successfully got rid of the virus, there are a few final steps to take.

1 Restart your computer and look for errors.

2 Run a new virus scan to verify the virus has gone.

3 If the virus was spread to you via email, contact people you know and warn them that they may also be infected.

4 If you disabled System Restore, enable it.

5 Connect to the internet to update your virus definitions.

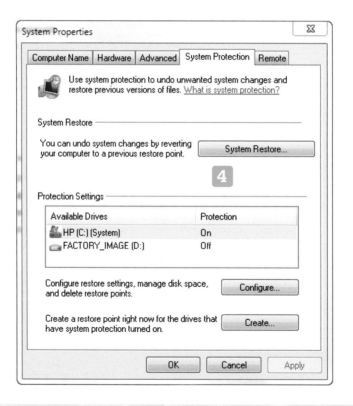

ALERT: If you've worked through this chapter and still have the virus, you may have to format and reinstall your computer.

HOT TIP: If you still have the virus but have not taken the computer to a repair shop, do so (unless you want to reinstall the computer yourself, or continue to try to resolve the issue).

13 Manage and share data

Introduction

You have to manage physical files and folders in a filing cabinet, and you also have to manage files and folders on your computer. With a filing cabinet, perhaps you share the physical key to the cabinet; in Windows 7, you share files and folders digitally, often using passwords. And as with a physical filing cabinet you have to occasionally get rid of stuff you no longer need, move files, copy files and even find missing files. In this chapter you'll learn all you need to know to get started with successfully managing the digital data you've amassed on your PC.

Review sharing settings

As you learned in Chapter 7, your network should be private (set to either Home or Work, not Public). Additionally, you must give permission for other computers and users to view, sign in and/or access the data on it. All of this is easily configured in the Network and Sharing Center. Here's a quick recap of what we discussed in Chapter 7.

1 Open the Network and Sharing Center.

2 Verify your Network is set to Home (or Work). If it's set to Public, change it.

3 Click Change advanced sharing settings.

4 Enable the desired sharing settings.

5 Click Save changes if applicable.

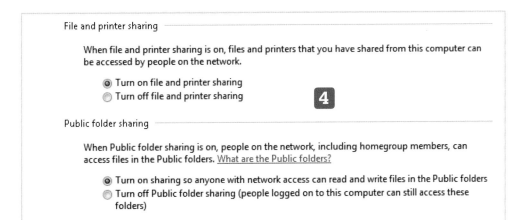

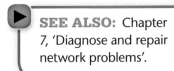

> **SEE ALSO:** Chapter 7, 'Diagnose and repair network problems'.

> **! ALERT:** It's best to set your home network to Home (not Work). Homegroups can only be configured when the network type is Home.

> **HOT TIP:** You should keep three security features in place: your network should be set to Home (or Work), your router should be configured with a password, and anyone connected to the network should be assigned a user name and password on your computer to access the data on it.

Create a folder

Your personal folders will suit your needs for a while, but you may want to create folders of your own. You can create an entirely new folder on the desktop to hold information you access often, and in addition you can create subfolders inside folders that already exist.

1 To create a folder on the desktop:
   a. Right-click an empty area on the desktop.
   b. Point to New.
   c. Click Folder.
   d. Type a name for the folder.
   e. Press Enter on the keyboard.

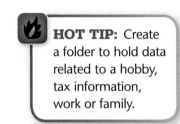

HOT TIP: Create a folder to hold data related to a hobby, tax information, work or family.

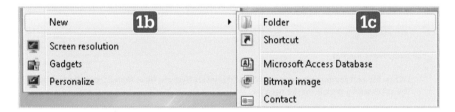

2 To create a subfolder in any existing folder:
   a. Click New folder.
   b. Type a name for the folder.
   c. Press Enter on the keyboard.

3 Press Enter on the keyboard.

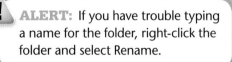

ALERT: If you have trouble typing a name for the folder, right-click the folder and select Rename.

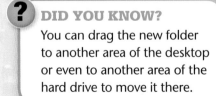

DID YOU KNOW?
You can drag the new folder to another area of the desktop or even to another area of the hard drive to move it there.

Move or copy data into a folder

Folders contain files and subfolders. Sometimes you'll need to copy a file or subfolder to another location. Perhaps you want to copy data to an external drive, memory card or USB thumb drive for the purpose of backing it up. Alternatively, you may want to move the file to another location.

1 Locate a file or folder to copy (or move).

2 Right-click the file or folder.

3 While holding down the right mouse key, drag the file or folder to the new location.

4 Drop it there.

5 Choose Copy here or Move here.

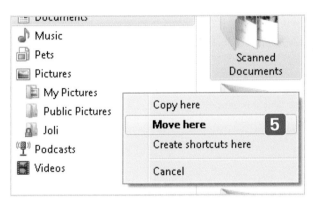

HOT TIP: It's okay that the pop-up says 'Move to ...' when you're dragging with the right mouse key depressed. When you let go of that key, you'll have the option to move or to copy.

DID YOU KNOW?
It may be helpful to think of folders and subfolders in a more physical way, as folders and subfolders in a filing cabinet. Folders on your computer help you keep data organised and easily available, just as you would in a filing cabinet.

Delete a file or folder

When you are sure you no longer need a particular file, you can delete it. Deleting sends the file to the Recycle Bin. This file can be 'restored' if you decide you need it later, provided you have not emptied the Recycle Bin since deleting it.

1 Locate a file or folder to delete.

2 Right-click the file or folder.

3 Choose Delete.

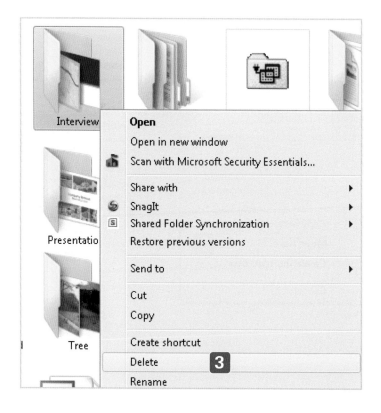

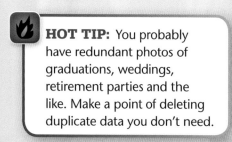 **HOT TIP:** You probably have redundant photos of graduations, weddings, retirement parties and the like. Make a point of deleting duplicate data you don't need.

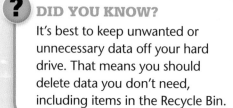 **DID YOU KNOW?**
It's best to keep unwanted or unnecessary data off your hard drive. That means you should delete data you don't need, including items in the Recycle Bin.

Share a file or folder

If you've turned on sharing options, some of your data is already shared. If you've enabled Public Sharing and use the Public folders, you've streamlined the process. Sometimes, though, you need to share a folder that's 'outside' of the default sharing settings, such as a folder you've created on your desktop.

1 Right-click a folder you want to share. (Choose one that is not currently shared via other options.)

2 Click Share with.

3 If you've set up a homegroup, select an appropriate sharing option.

4 If you don't have a homegroup, click Specific people and work through the next section.

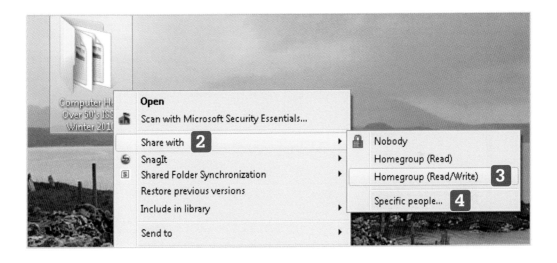

Configure specific sharing permissions

You may want to share a specific folder with your spouse but not with your grandchild who also accesses the computer. You can apply specific permissions to personalise who gets to see what.

1 Perform the steps in the previous section.

2 In the File Sharing window, click the down arrow under Add.

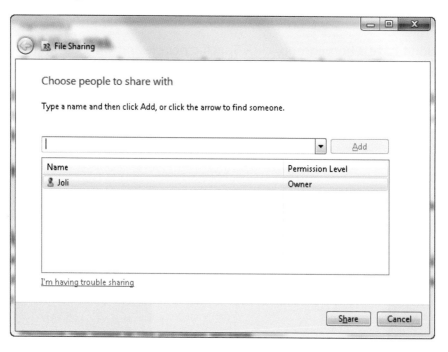

3 Select the person to share with.

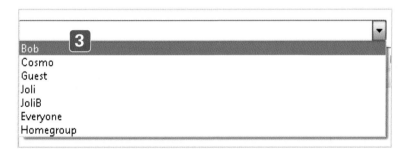

4 Click Add.

5 Click the arrow next to the new user and select the appropriate permission.

6 Click Share and then Done.

ALERT: If you don't see the person you want to share with in the drop-down list, you'll need to create a user account for them on your computer.

HOT TIP: Note that you can select the option to share with Everyone. If you're going to do that, consider simply moving the folder to something already shared, such as the Pictures or Documents folder, or one of the Public folders.

Understand libraries

Libraries contain access to data in their Public and private counterparts. For instance, the Pictures library offers access to the data in the My Pictures folder as well as the data from the Public Pictures folder. There are four libraries: Documents, Pictures, Music and Videos.

1 Click Start and click Documents.

2 Position your mouse in the left pane beside Documents.

3 Click the down arrow.

4 Click Public Documents to view the contents of each folder.

▶ **SEE ALSO:** 'Move or copy data into a folder', earlier in this chapter.

 **HOT TIP:** If you learn how to save your data in library folders and to access data through those libraries, your backups will be easier to create and more complete, sharing your data will be easier, and data will be easier to find.

HOT TIP: Move all data to their appropriate library folders.

Create a new library

There are only four libraries but you can add your own. You may want to create a library named Pets, Hobbies, Fundraisers or something similar. This will enable you to access all data related to that topic in one place.

1 Click Start and then Documents.

2 Click Libraries to see the four default libraries.

3 Right-click Libraries, click New and click Library.

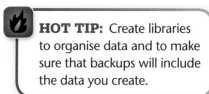

HOT TIP: Create libraries to organise data and to make sure that backups will include the data you create.

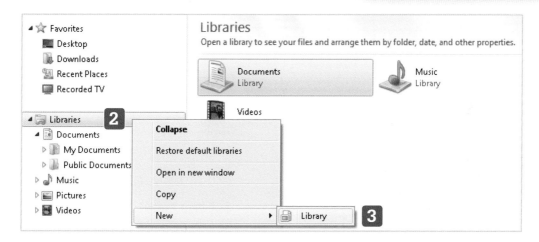

4 Name the library and click Enter on the keyboard.

5 In the left pane, click the new library.

6 Click Include a folder.

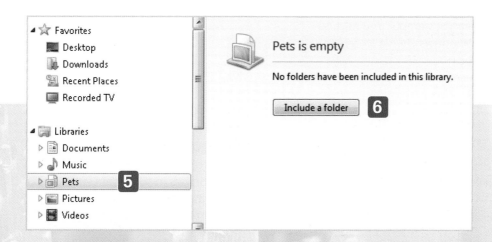

7 Browse to a folder to include and click it once.

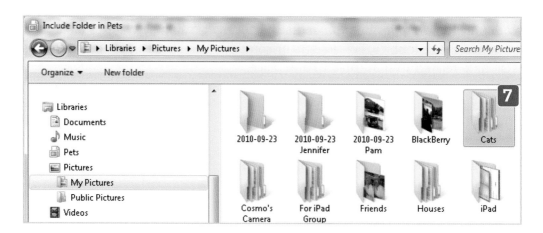

8 Click Include folder.

9 To add folders to the new library:

   a. Click 1 location.

   b. Click Add.

   c. Repeat Steps 7 and 8 and click OK.

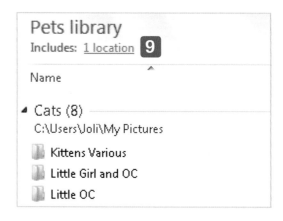

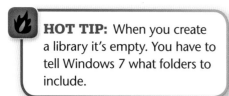
HOT TIP: When you create a library it's empty. You have to tell Windows 7 what folders to include.

DID YOU KNOW?
Windows Backup and Restore automatically backs up data in libraries.

HOT TIP: You can also create libraries in Public libraries to share data with others on your home network.

Find a missing file or folder

After you create data you save it to your hard drive. When you're ready to use the file again, you have to locate it and open it. If you know the document is in the Documents folder, you can click Start and then click Documents. Then, you can simply double-click the file to open it. However, if you aren't sure where the file is, you'll have to search for it.

1 Click Start.

2 In the Start Search window, type the name of the file.

3 Click the file to open it. There will be multiple search results.

4 If you don't see what you're looking for, click See more results.

5 Scan the results to locate the file.

> **! ALERT:** If you don't know the exact name of the file, you can type part of the name or even a word in a file.

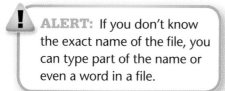

HOT TIP: In the Search Results window you can filter the results from the top right search window. Click to see the options.

? DID YOU KNOW?

If you don't know any part of the name of the file, you can type a word that is included inside the file or a specific type of file.

Restore data from the Recycle Bin

If you delete something that you later decide you want to keep or need, you can 'restore' it from the Recycle Bin. That is, unless you've emptied the Recycle Bin since deleting the item!

1 Double-click the Recycle Bin.

2 Right-click the file, shortcut, folder or data to recover.

3 Click Restore.

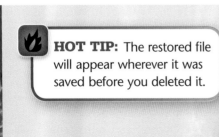
HOT TIP: The restored file will appear wherever it was saved before you deleted it.

ALERT: If you empty the Recycle Bin you won't be able to restore any data previously in it.

Create a search folder

A search folder is a 'live' folder that is updated every time you open it. If you are always adding data related to your grandkids, say, and you name the data or tag it so Windows 7 can recognise it for what it is, you can create a Search folder to keep an updated grouping of that data.

1 Think of a name, topic, hobby, holiday or something equally unique to base your search on.

2 Click Start and type that word.

3 Click See more results.

4 Click Save search.

5 Accept the name or change it and click Save (not shown).

6 The new search folder will appear under Favorites in the Explorer window.

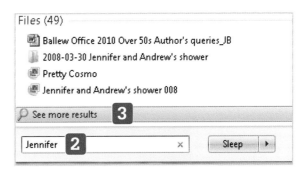

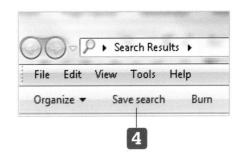

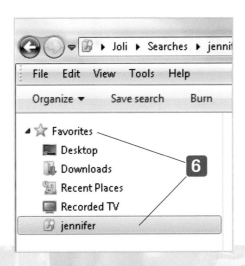

ALERT: Windows 7 can't classify a picture named, say, IMG001_234B as a picture of your grandchild. You will have to rename that image (and others) to something more recognisable, such as Jennifer_12_13_2010.

? DID YOU KNOW?

When you create a Search folder, no data is moved. You simply have access to all the related data in a single place.

Remove the Read-only attribute

Files have attributes. One attribute is the Read-only attribute. You can't edit a file if it's read-only. Thus, if you ever receive a message that a file can't be edited, you must remove that attribute.

1 Right-click the problem file and click Properties.

2 Deselect Read-only.

3 Click OK.

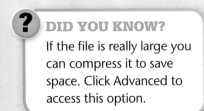

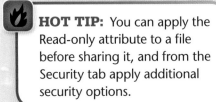

? DID YOU KNOW?
If the file is really large you can compress it to save space. Click Advanced to access this option.

HOT TIP: You can apply the Read-only attribute to a file before sharing it, and from the Security tab apply additional security options.

14 Fix problems with media

Introduction

If you play media on your computer, chances are you've run into a few problems. Maybe a song that used to play won't play any more, or maybe you can't access a video stored on one computer from another on your network. If you use Media Center to record TV shows, you may have problems that stem from recording too much TV, and your hard drive is filling up with unwanted media. Perhaps you have a DVD that simply won't play, no matter what you try. There are all kinds of problems that can crop up. In this chapter we'll cover the most common.

Move media files into media libraries

You know when your home is disorganised, things can go wrong. You can't find what you need when you need it and neither can anyone else; this can cause problems. The same thing happens when your computer's media are disorganised. When Windows 7 can't find the media files you've saved, it can't offer them up for you to play.

1 Click Start and click Documents.

2 Look in the Documents library for media.

3 Move the media to the appropriate folder by dragging it there.

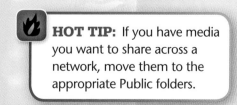

HOT TIP: If you have media you want to share across a network, move them to the appropriate Public folders.

4 Look in each of the other folders you see in the left pane.

5 Move any misplaced media into their appropriate folders.

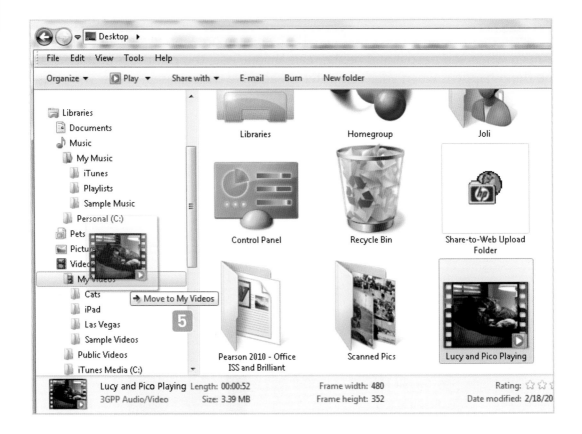

Clean up your media libraries

If you were to clean up the media in your home, you'd probably get rid of those old 8-track tapes and cassettes or convert them to something that will play. You might even consider throwing out (or gifting) some of the movies you used to like but don't any more. Just as you'd clean up your physical media, you should clean up your digital media.

1 Browse each media library, looking for media you no longer want.

2 Right-click any file to delete.

3 Click Delete.

4 Right-click any file to rename.

5 Click Rename and type a new name.

6 Press Enter on the keyboard.

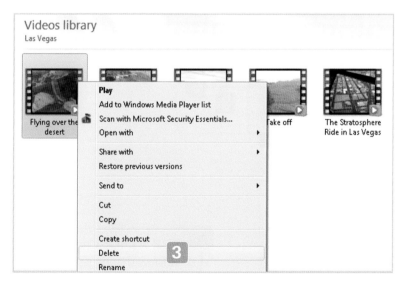

ALERT: Don't rename any folders that were named by a program. For instance, don't rename the iTunes Library. You want the original program to be able to find it.

HOT TIP: Review the other options from the right-click menu. Note you can send files, copy files and more.

Share media from Media Player

If you want to access media on one computer from another computer on your network, you have to tell Windows 7 you want to share it. You should verify this in two places: in Media Player and in the Network and Sharing Center. The latter is detailed in Chapter 7.

1 Open Media Player from the Start, All Programs menu.

2 Click the arrow next to Stream.

3 Tick Automatically allow devices to play my media.

4 Click Automatically allow all computers and devices (not shown).

5 Repeat steps 2–4 and click Allow remote control of my Player.

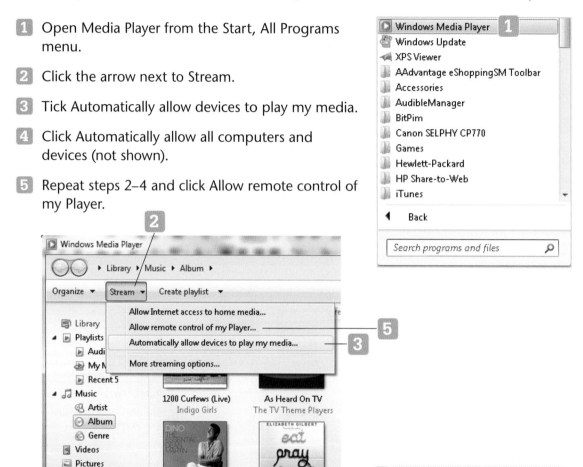

SEE ALSO: Chapter 7, 'Review sharing settings'.

 HOT TIP: Open the Network and Sharing Center, click Change advanced sharing settings and verify that Media streaming is turned on (for good measure).

Access media over your network

To access media from another computer, you have to be connected to the network and the computer that stores the media must be turned on. Of course, sharing has to be enabled on the computer that holds the media as well. If you're having problems, verify all of those things are enabled and functional.

1 On the remote computer, open Windows Media Player.

2 In the left pane, click the arrow by Other Libraries.

3 Click Artist, Album or Genre.

4 Click any song to play it.

! ALERT: The screen here shows a Windows 7 computer. If you are running Windows XP or Windows Vista, you'll see something different.

? DID YOU KNOW?

If you have two Windows 7 computers, they belong to a homegroup and you've enabled media streaming (sharing), you can right-click a file on one computer, click Play To and cause the file to play on the other.

Learn what program you need to play a file

Sometimes you'll have a file you can't play because you don't have the proper software to play it. You know that you can't play a cassette tape in a CD player, and likewise you won't be able to play, say, a file downloaded from Zune created for Zune software using iTunes or Windows Media Player.

1 Locate and double-click a file to play.

2 Select Use the Web service to find the correct program.

3 Click OK.

4 If you discover which program you need, download and install it.

5 If you can't find the program you need, perform a more thorough web search.

6 You may discover the files can be opened with iTunes, QuickTime or another program.

Windows

Windows can't open this file:

File: RelicUnabridgedPart1_mp332_Joli_Ballew.aa

To open this file, Windows needs to know what program you want to use to open it. Windows can go online to look it up automatically, or you can manually select from a list of programs that are installed on your computer.

What do you want to do?

○ Use the Web service to find the correct program **2**

○ Select a program from a list of installed programs

3 [OK]   [Cancel]

Program(s) that open AA files

Windows

- Audible AudibleManager
- Apple iTunes
- Nero Multimedia Suite 10
- RapidSolution Tunebite 7
- SoundTaxi Media Suite
- TuneCab

ALERT: Download programs only from reputable, reliable sites. Do not download registry scanners, error detectors, or any other third-party program. Be very careful!

SEE ALSO: If you find that you have the required software already, you'll need to tell Windows that you want to use that program to open the file from here on. See 'Associate a file type with a program', later in this chapter.

Obtain third-party media software

You learned how to obtain third-party software in Chapter 8. That's probably what will be required if you can't play a particular file type. You'll probably need iTunes, QuickTime, or software associated with an MP3 player, such as Zune.

1 Figure out what software you need: see previous section.

2 Locate the manufacturer's website:

   a. For iTunes, visit www.apple.com/itunes.

   b. For Zune, visit www.zune.net.

   c. For QuickTime, visit www.apple.com/quicktime.

3 Follow the download and installation instructions.

4 Register and log on (but only if you have to).

> ▶ **SEE ALSO:** Chapter 8, 'Install missing and must-have applications'.

> ⚠ **ALERT:** When you first start a program such as iTunes or QuickTime, it will prompt you to use it as the default player. Don't do that just yet.

> ⚠ **ALERT:** Again, do not download registry scanners, error-fixers or run any 'virus scans' from third-party sites. These are always scams and can harm your computer!

> ❓ **DID YOU KNOW?**
> Files meant for iTunes, Zune, Audible and the like are often 'protected'. You may have to log in with valid credentials to play them or authorise your computer using your personal iTunes, Audible or Zune account.

Associate a file type with a program

You can tell Windows what program you prefer to use for specific file types. For instance, iTunes can play Audible files, as can Media Player and Media Center. To configure a specific program to open other than the default, you must associate the file type with a program. Here we'll associate a program with a file that currently won't play when double-clicked.

1 Double-click the file that won't play.

2 Click Select a program from a list of installed programs.

3 Click OK.

4 Select the program to use and click OK.

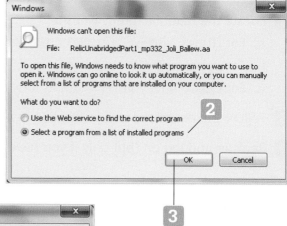

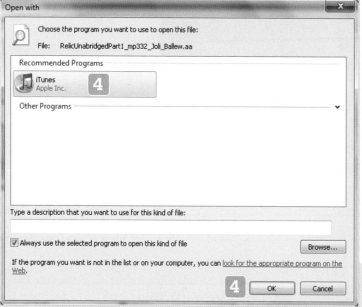

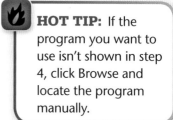

HOT TIP: If the program you want to use isn't shown in step 4, click Browse and locate the program manually.

HOT TIP: If you get an error stating you need to reinstall the program, say iTunes, do so.

Set multiple file associations

You can set multiple file associations at one time and tell Windows how you want media to play. For instance, you may want to play audio books in iTunes and music in Media Player.

1 Click Start and type Associations.

2 In the results, click Make a file type always open in a specific program.

3 Locate the type of file to change.

4 Click Change program.

5 Select the desired program, then click OK.

6 Repeat as desired and click Close.

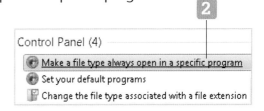

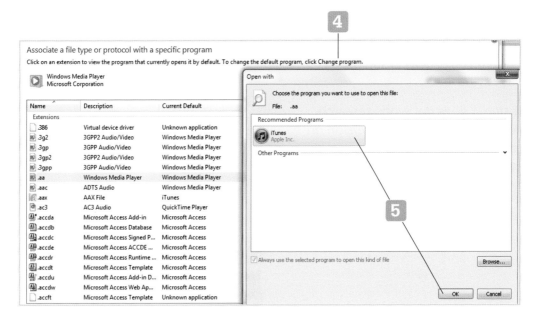

HOT TIP: We suggest you use a file's native program to open it.

DID YOU KNOW?
If the program isn't listed in the screen shown in the second figure, you can click Browse to locate it.

DID YOU KNOW?
You can also right-click any media file and click Properties to access the option to open the file in another program.

Convert files to another format

It is possible to convert a file from one format to another. For instance, you can convert Audible files to MP3 files and thus play them on any MP3 player. (As it stands, Audible files can play only on iPods and other compatible players, and cannot be played on, say, a Sony Walkman.)

1 Find a media file's file type:
   a. Right-click the file.
   b. Click Properties.
   c. Note the file type.
   d. Click Cancel.

2 Decide what type of file you want to convert to (Audible to MP3, perhaps).

3 See whether you can perform the desired conversion in software you already have.

4 If step 3 does not work, research how to perform the conversion on the internet, or visit a local computer store.

5 Purchase, install and run the required software.

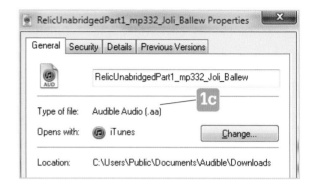

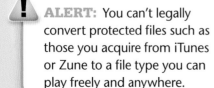

ALERT: You can't legally convert protected files such as those you acquire from iTunes or Zune to a file type you can play freely and anywhere.

HOT TIP: I feel that if you purchase an audiobook or an entire album and you own it, you should be within your rights to convert the file to a format that will play on your Sony Walkman or other MP3 player. So if you want my personal blessing, you have it.

Troubleshoot DVD playback

On occasion, you'll put a DVD in the DVD drive and nothing will happen. The movie doesn't play, or it starts to play but a problem arises. There are several things that could be wrong and several ways to troubleshoot.

- Insert a previously played DVD to rule out the possibility that the DVD drive is damaged.
- If another DVD plays, verify the DVD you're trying to play is clean and is not scratched or damaged.
- Try the DVD in another DVD player to see whether the DVD is damaged.
- Reduce or increase your computer's resolution in the Control Panel's Display settings.
- If you see errors that denote a missing 'decoder', you'll have to acquire the appropriate decoder to resolve the problem.

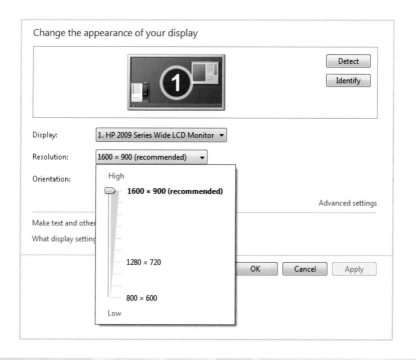

ALERT: When searching for a decoder, visit a reputable website and read all the reviews before making a purchase.

 HOT TIP: You should be able to play most DVDs on your computer. If you can't they may be illegal or bootlegged.

Change record settings in Media Center

You need to read this section only if you record TV shows in Windows Media Center. The main problem associated with this is that your hard drive can fill up with shows you don't know you're recording. By default, Windows Media Center records all instances of a TV show, including reruns.

1 Open Media Center.

2 Scroll down to Tasks and click settings.

3 Click TV, Recorder and then Recording Defaults (not shown).

4 Review each setting. Consider changing the default setting to record new shows and reruns to only New.

5 Scroll down to Keep up to: and select a finite number.

6 Click Save.

? DID YOU KNOW?
The only limit set initially on how many shows Media Center will record is the size of your hard drive.

🔥 HOT TIP: If you're constantly missing out on the last few minutes of a show because it overruns, change the setting for Stop when possible to two minutes.

! ALERT: If you're recording a show that's been off the air for a while, keep the New & rerun setting.

15 Manage and maintain your PC

Introduction

You may not have any computer problems that you know of, or by now you've rid your computer of the ones you had. However, just as you'd maintain a car or a home, you also have to maintain your computer. In that vein, we've put together a list of things you can do to avoid future problems and to keep your machine running at peak performance.

Delete unwanted data

You know how to delete data, so this section is simply a reminder to do it on a regular basis. You have to take out the rubbish each week at home and you must take out the rubbish regularly on your computer too.

1 Locate a file or folder to delete.

2 Right-click it.

3 Click Delete.

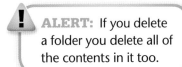

ALERT: If you delete a folder you delete all of the contents in it too.

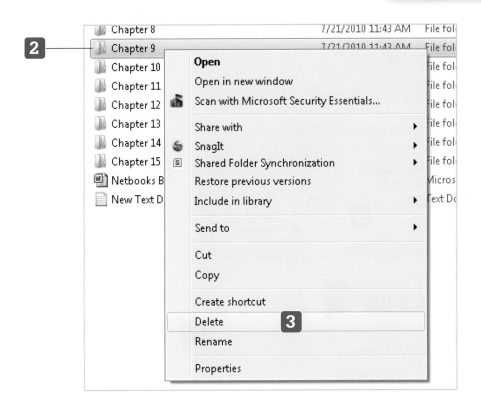

DID YOU KNOW?
Some files and folders have an arrow included with them and are thus 'shortcuts' to the data. If you delete the shortcut you do not delete the data.

HOT TIP: Hold down the Ctrl key while selecting data to select additional files or folders.

Compress files and folders

With today's big hard drives, you probably won't run out of hard drive space unless you have a lot of media files. It's always better to be safe than sorry though. If you have data you haven't used for a long time, consider compressing it – it will take up less space on your hard drive.

1 Locate a folder that contains data you rarely access.

2 Right-click it.

3 Choose Send to, and then Compressed (zipped) folder.

4 After the compression tasks have finished, name the folder.

5 Press Enter on the keyboard.

 HOT TIP: When you compress a folder in this manner, you create a new, compressed folder that contains the data in the existing non-compressed folder. You can now delete the non-compressed files, if desired, and move the newly compressed file off the computer to a DVD or external hard drive.

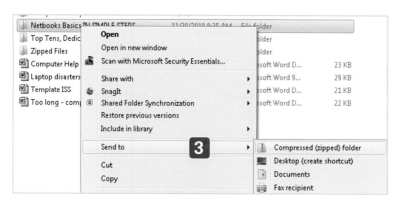

 DID YOU KNOW?
Compressed folders can end up being a fraction of the size of their originals.

WHAT DOES THIS MEAN?
Compressing: compressed files take up less hard drive space than non-compressed files. You can work with compressed files and folders in the same way as you do with uncompressed files and folders. You can compress virtually anything, including pictures, videos, music and documents.

Move rarely used data off of your PC

If you have data on your PC that you rarely use, consider moving it off of the computer and onto another, or to an external hard drive (or both). This will enable you to free up hard drive space on your PC, while also keeping the data available if you need it.

1 Connect to the external hard drive, network drive or other computer.

2 Consider positioning the windows side by side so you can see both.

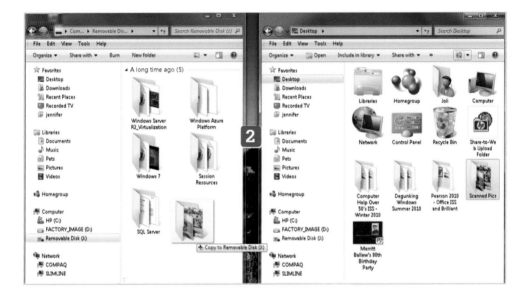

3 Drag the folder to move to the external drive.

4 Drop it there and click Move here.

Organise your files in folders

Think about how hard it is to keep a junk drawer, toolbox, garage or basement organised. It's just as hard to keep a computer organised. This is because you continually use and amass *stuff*. In the case of a computer, this *stuff* consists of digital files, email, pictures, music, videos and more. It's important to try to stay organised!

- Move misplaced data into its appropriate folder.
- Create subfolders in the default folders to organise data.
- Move data into respective subfolders.

Merritt Ballew's 90th
Birthday Party

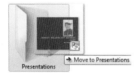

Presentations

→ Move to Presentations

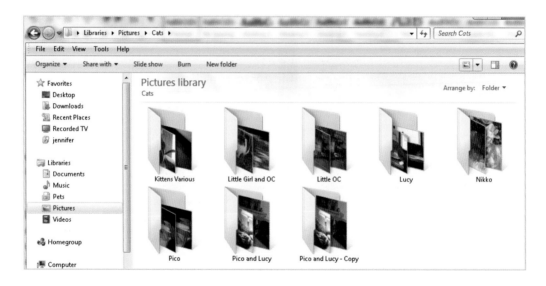

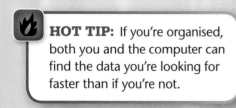

HOT TIP: If you're organised, both you and the computer can find the data you're looking for faster than if you're not.

HOT TIP: Every time you acquire new data, save it to the proper folder.

Enable the Guest account

When you have guests, they may ask to use your computer to email, upload and print pictures, write and print letters, and perform other tasks. To protect your data and keep the computer safe from unintentional harm, enable the Guest account while you have a visitor.

1 Click Start and click Control Panel.

2 Click Add or remove user accounts.

3 Click Guest.

4 Click Turn On.

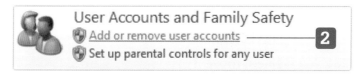

Do you want to turn on the guest account?

If you turn on the guest account, people who do not have an account can use the guest account to log on to the computer. Password-protected files, folders, or settings are not accessible to guest users.

ALERT: Disable the Guest account immediately after your guests leave. It can be a security loophole for hackers.

? DID YOU KNOW?
Guests who log on using the Guest account can't do anything that would harm the computer, but they can save data, use programs you've installed, surf the internet and more.

Keep your desktop clean

Your computer's desktop will get cluttered just like your physical desktop. If your computer's desktop is crowded and disorganised, it'll take you longer to find what you want there (just as it does on a physical desktop). Once a month or so, take inventory and get rid of (or move) items that do not belong.

- If an icon has an arrow on it, it's a shortcut. Right-click to delete it safely.

- If an icon does not have an arrow on it and it's something you created, move it to the appropriate folder.

- If the icon is a system icon, such as Control Panel, Computer, Network or similar you can safely delete it.

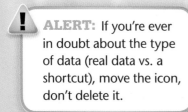
ALERT: If you're ever in doubt about the type of data (real data vs. a shortcut), move the icon, don't delete it.

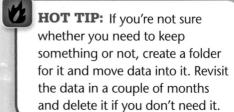
HOT TIP: If you're not sure whether you need to keep something or not, create a folder for it and move data into it. Revisit the data in a couple of months and delete it if you don't need it.

Pin items to the Start menu or taskbar

If you find you're spending a lot of time clicking Start, then All Programs and then the program you want to use, you can place an icon for the program on the Start menu or the taskbar. This is called 'pinning'.

1 Locate the icon for the program you want to pin.

2 Right-click the icon and choose:
   a. Pin to Taskbar.
   b. Pin to Start Menu.

3 Note the new icon.

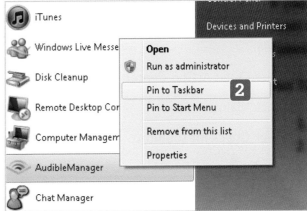

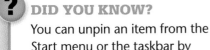

HOT TIP: When an item is pinned, say, to the taskbar, it's always available with a single click.

? DID YOU KNOW?
You can unpin an item from the Start menu or the taskbar by right-clicking it and choosing the appropriate option.

HOT TIP: You can right-click any icon on the taskbar to access its 'jump list', which offers quick access to recent files, among other things.

Review problem reports and solutions

Some things have maintenance programs built in and offer warnings when things go awry (like the dashboard lights on your car). Windows 7 has the Action Center, which is constantly watching for problems and looking for solutions. You should check for solutions often, perhaps once a month.

1 Click the flag icon in the Notification area.

2 Click Open Action Center.

3 Click Maintenance.

4 Click Check for solutions.

5 If solutions are found, consider applying those solutions as instructed.

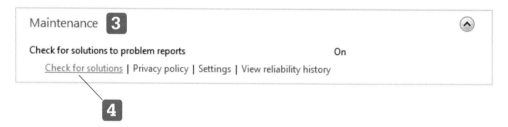

HOT TIP: While in the Action Center, click View performance information in the left pane (not shown here) to see how you can improve performance.

ALERT: Not all suggestions you'll find in the Action Center need to be performed or applied. For instance, if you don't use your telephone modem but a new driver has been found, there's no reason to download and install the driver.

Keep your computer up to date

You installed anti-virus software and you should verify it is updating itself regularly. Windows 7 offers Windows Update, and that should be enabled and updating automatically as well. Additionally, you should perform regular backups to keep your data safe. Here are a few other things you can do to stay up to date.

- Run Disk Cleanup once a month.
- Empty the Sent and Deleted items folders in your email program once every three months (saving the last two or three months of data in case you need to reference it).
- Run performance tests three times a year (in the Control Panel).

Component	What is rated	Subscore	Base score
Processor:	Calculations per second	5.6	
Memory (RAM):	Memory operations per second	5.5	
Graphics:	Desktop performance for Windows Aero	3.3	3.2
Gaming graphics:	3D business and gaming graphics performance	3.2	Determined by lowest subscore
Primary hard disk:	Disk data transfer rate	5.9	

? What do these numbers mean?

? Tips for improving your computer's performance.

View and print detailed performance and system information

- Check the Action Center weekly.
- Run virus scans weekly.

 HOT TIP: Use canned air once a year to blow dust out of the inside of the case. You will need to open the case, so research the best way to do that first, or take your computer to a trusted friend or relative.

 ALERT: Make sure your computer is physically placed where it has necessary air circulation to keep it from overheating.

16 Install hardware to improve performance

Introduction

If you've discovered that additional hardware would improve the performance of your PC, or if it would make your life easier or make you more efficient, you probably need a few tips on how to install it. Of course, you can plug in brand new printers and scanners and install the entire CD or DVD that came with them or you can be a bit savvier about it, installing only what's actually necessary.

Additionally, you may find that you would rather make an older piece of equipment work, one that does not have an installation disk or does not currently work the way it should. In these cases, you need to find a 'driver' and install it. A driver is a piece of software (or code) that allows the device to communicate with Windows 7 and vice versa.

Finally, you may want to improve the performance of your PC without opening the computer tower. You can do this with a USB flash drive and ReadyBoost.

Install a digital camera, webcam or media card

You know how to install hardware. However, you can do better and prevent future problems by performing installations in a new way. Follow along here to find out how to perform the best installation possible.

1 Connect the camera to a wall outlet or insert fresh batteries and connect the camera to the PC using either a USB cable or a FireWire cable.

2 Insert the CD for the device, if you have it; if a pop-up message appears, click the X to close the window.

3 Turn on the camera. Place it in Playback mode if that exists. Often, simply turning on the camera is enough.

4 Wait while the driver is installed.

5 You'll see the camera in the Computer window (click Start, click Computer).

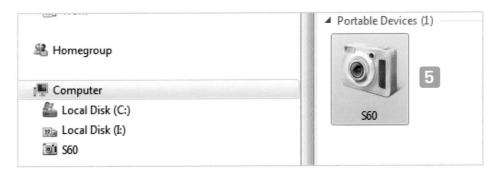

! ALERT: It's usually best to connect a new camera, turn it on and let Windows 7 install it. You need to intervene only when Windows 7 can't install the hardware on its own.

? DID YOU KNOW?
When you install everything on the CD that comes with your camera, you're probably installing applications you'll never use and don't need.

! ALERT: If the camera does not install properly, only then should you install the CD or DVD that came with the camera.

Install a printer

Most of the time, adding a printer is as easy as installing a camera. You plug it in and turn it on, then wait for Windows 7 to install it. You'll install scanners, mobile phones and other hardware similarly. If need be, you can install the software that came with it; however, often this is unnecessary.

1 Connect the printer to a wall outlet.

2 Connect the printer to the PC using the appropriate cable.

3 Insert the CD for the device, if you have it.

4 If a pop-up message appears regarding the CD, click the X to close the window.

5 Turn on the device and wait while the driver is installed.

6 Locate the new printer in the Devices and Printers window (from the Start menu).

Your devices are ready to use
Device driver software installed successfully.

5

ALERT: Always remain aware of what you're installing. Install drivers only, then install software if you find you need it.

? DID YOU KNOW?
Leave the CD in the drive. If Windows 7 wants information on the CD, it will acquire it from there.

HOT TIP: You will need to install the printer software if you want to access advanced printer preferences such as printing in reverse or applying light or heavy ink.

Install software

Hardware you buy almost always comes with a CD or DVD. It's called an installation disk. This disk often contains a driver *and* software. If Windows 7 can't install the driver itself, you'll need to install the driver from the disk. If, after installing the driver, the hardware still doesn't function properly, you'll need to install the software.

1 Insert the CD or DVD in the appropriate drive. If prompted. click Run or Install.

2 If you are not prompted:

    a. Click Start.

    b. Click Computer.

    c. Right-click the CD or DVD drive.

    d. Click Install or run program from your media.

3 Work through the installation wizard.

ALERT: If you leave the CD or DVD in the drive while Windows is trying to install the device, it'll pull only what it needs from the disk (the driver) and nothing else.

HOT TIP: You may need to install the software for a printer or scanner, but most of the time Windows Live Photo Gallery (rather than the camera software) is the best option for a camera.

Change when the computer sleeps

Your computer is configured to go to sleep after a specific period of idle time. If you do not want your computer to go to sleep, for instance if Media Center is supposed to record something in the middle of the night, you can change this behaviour.

1 Click Start and in the Start Search window type Power.

2 In the results, under Programs, click Power Options.

3 Click Change when the computer sleeps.

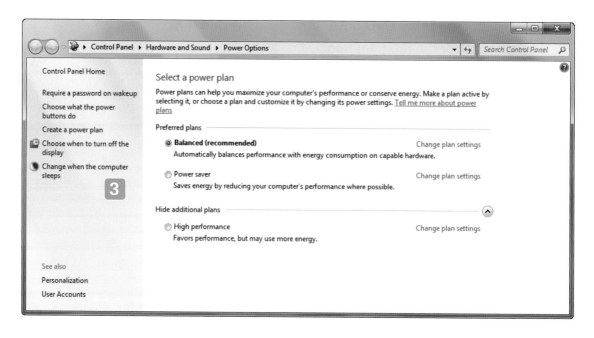

4 Use the drop-down lists to make changes as desired.

5 Click Save changes.

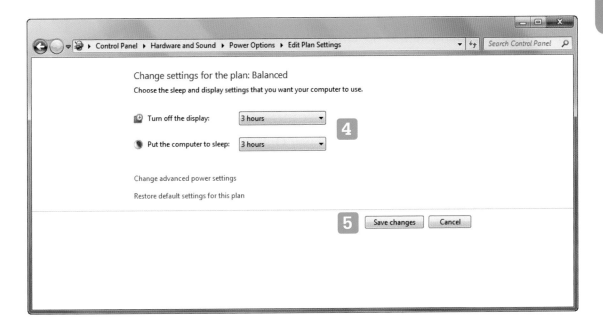

Control Panel ▸ Hardware and Sound ▸ Power Options ▸ Edit Plan Settings

Search Control Panel

Change settings for the plan: Balanced
Choose the sleep and display settings that you want your computer to use.

Turn off the display: 3 hours

Put the computer to sleep: 3 hours

4

Change advanced power settings

Restore default settings for this plan

5 Save changes   Cancel

 HOT TIP: If your computer is fairly new, Media Center may be able to wake up to record a TV show. Test it to find out.

 DID YOU KNOW?
You can restore the sleep defaults by clicking Restore default settings for this plan.

Change what happens when you press the Power button

Your computer is configured to do something specific when you press the Power button. By default, this is to shut down the computer, but you can change this behaviour.

1 Click Start and in the Start Search window type Power.

2 In the results, under Programs, click Power Options.

3 Click Choose what the power buttons do.

4 Use the drop-down lists to make changes as desired.

5 Click Save changes.

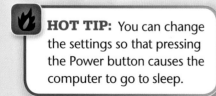

HOT TIP: You can change the settings so that pressing the Power button causes the computer to go to sleep.

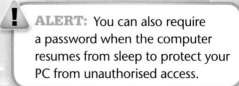

ALERT: You can also require a password when the computer resumes from sleep to protect your PC from unauthorised access.

Top 10 computer problems solved

Problem 1: There's something wrong with my computer. It was fine yesterday

System Restore regularly creates and saves *restore points* that contain information about your computer that Windows uses to work properly. If your computer starts acting strangely, you can use System Restore to restore it to a time when the computer was working properly. It's like turning back time!

1 Open System Restore. (Use the Start Search window to locate it.)

2 Click Next to accept and apply the recommended restore point.

3 Click Finish.

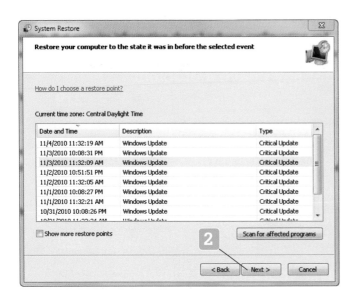

DID YOU KNOW?
Because System Restore works only with its own system files, running System Restore will not affect any of your personal data. Your pictures, email, documents, music, etc. will not be deleted or changed.

ALERT: If running System Restore on a laptop, make sure it's plugged in. System Restore should never be interrupted.

WHAT DOES THIS MEAN?

Restore point: a snapshot of the Registry and system state that can be used to make an unstable computer stable again.

Registry: a part of the operating system that contains information about hardware configuration and settings, user configuration and preferences, software configuration and preferences, and other system-specific information.

Problem 2: I have a piece of hardware that recently stopped working or responding

Common problems that occur with malfunctioning hardware are that the device is turned off and needs to be turned on, a cable has been damaged by a frisky cat or run over and damaged by a wheeled chair, or a scanner has gone to 'sleep' and needs to be turned off and on again to wake it up. But there can be other issues.

- If the device is not recognised in the Devices and Printers window, the problem could be any of the following:
  - Media cards have been inadvertently protected by a slider that's been moved from off to on.
  - Hardware has been plugged into a non-working electrical outlet or connected to a non-working USB port on the computer.
  - The device has frozen up and you need to turn it off and then turn back on.
  - The device isn't properly connected.
  - The device isn't in the proper mode, is out of ink or paper, or is otherwise damaged.

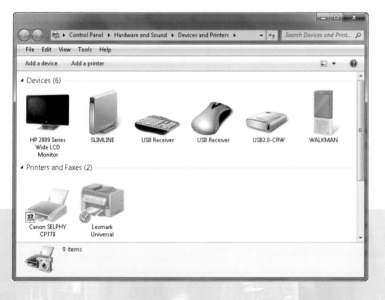

 HOT TIP: Hardware such as wireless mice and keyboards will stop working when their batteries die.

 HOT TIP: You can't print to a printer that's disconnected from the computer or turned off.

 ALERT: If your device does not appear in the Devices and Printers window, Windows can't use it.

Problem 3: How can I be sure that my computer is up to date and protected from the latest security threats?

Windows Update offers the easiest way to ensure that your computer is as up to date as possible, at least as far as patching security flaws Microsoft uncovers, having access to the latest features and obtaining updates to the operating system itself. If you're having problems, get the latest updates.

1 Click Start.

2 Click Control Panel.

3 Click System and Security.

4 Click Windows Update.

5 In the left pane, click Change settings.

6 Configure the settings as shown here and click OK.

Adjust your computer's settings

System and Security
Review your computer's status
Back up your computer
Find and fix problems

Control Panel Home

Check for updates

Change settings

View update history

Restore hidden updates

Updates: frequently asked questions

Choose how Windows can install updates

When your computer is online, Windows can automatically check for important updates and install them using these settings. When new updates are available, you can also install them before shutting down the computer.

How does automatic updating help me?

Important updates

Install updates automatically (recommended)

Install new updates: Every day at 3:00 AM

Recommended updates

☑ Give me recommended updates the same way I receive important updates

Who can install updates

☑ Allow all users to install updates on this computer 6

Microsoft Update

☑ Give me updates for Microsoft products and check for new optional Microsoft software when I update Windows

Software notifications

☐ Show me detailed notifications when new Microsoft software is available

Note: Windows Update might update itself automatically first when checking for other updates. Read our privacy statement online.

6 OK   Cancel

HOT TIP: Windows Update runs behind the scenes and you'll rarely notice it. Occasionally though, after an update, the computer will need to be rebooted.

ALERT: You may see that optional components or updates are available. You can view these updates and install them if desired.

DID YOU KNOW?
If the computer is not online at 3am, it will check for updates the next time it is.

Problem 4: I keep seeing pop-ups that say I have a problem with my computer

Windows 7 tries hard to take care of your PC and your data. You'll see a pop-up if your anti-virus software is out of date (or not installed), if you don't have the proper security settings configured, or if Windows Update is disabled. When you see alerts, pay attention! You'll want to resolve them.

1 Open the Action Center.

2 If there's anything in red or yellow, click the down arrow (if necessary) to see the problem.

3 Click the suggestion button to view the resolution and perform the task. Here, that's Options.

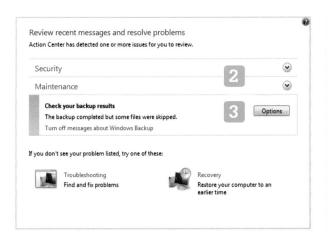

Problem 5: I can't connect to the internet

You'll be amazed at just how often restarting your computer will resolve a problem. After rebooting, if the problem is not resolved, you can try other solutions. If your problem is that your computer cannot connect to the internet, you can reboot the computer *and* the network hardware.

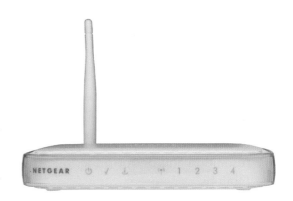

1 Turn off the PC and turn off and unplug the modem and router (as applicable).

2 If the modem has a battery backup, remove the battery.

 3 After a minute or so, reinsert the battery, plug in the modem, and turn it on.

4 After the modem has finished initialising, turn on the router, switch or hub.

5 After that device has finished initialising, turn on the PC.

SEE ALSO: Chapter 7 is all about resolving network and internet problems. However, rebooting everything is always a good first step. Refer to that chapter if this does not resolve your problem.

HOT TIP: The modem has finished initialising after all of its lights have stopped blinking.

 HOT TIP: Many problems occur due to loose or disconnected cables. A mouse can't work unless it's plugged in or its wireless component is. A cable modem can't work unless it's connected securely to the computer and the wall. When troubleshooting, always check your connections.

 DID YOU KNOW?

Often, you can disconnect, turn off and turn back on a peripheral such as a printer or scanner to resolve hardware problems quickly.

Problem 6: Every time I open or use a specific third-party program, something bad happens to my data

Programs that don't run properly may work better in Compatibility Mode, detailed in Chapter 5. If that doesn't work though, programs that cause perpetual problems should be uninstalled. They can cause system-wide problems that can be hard to diagnose.

1 Click Start, then click Control Panel.

2 Click Uninstall a program.

3 Locate the program in the list.

4 Click it and click Uninstall. (It might also have Change beside it.)

Programs
Uninstall a program **2**

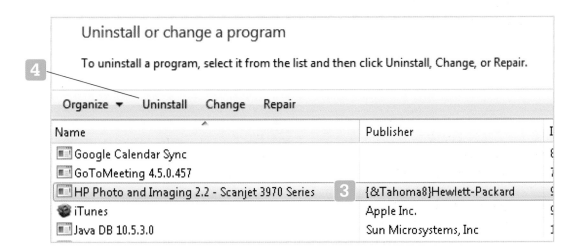

Uninstall or change a program

4 To uninstall a program, select it from the list and then click Uninstall, Change, or Repair.

Organize ▼   Uninstall   Change   Repair

Name	Publisher	I
Google Calendar Sync		8
GoToMeeting 4.5.0.457		7
HP Photo and Imaging 2.2 - Scanjet 3970 Series **3**	{&Tahoma8}Hewlett-Packard	9
iTunes	Apple Inc.	9
Java DB 10.5.3.0	Sun Microsystems, Inc	1

HOT TIP: When you uninstall a program you also keep it from potentially running in the background and using system resources.

? DID YOU KNOW?
Most programs that cause problems are too old to run well on a Windows 7 computer.

Problem 7: My computer won't boot up. I can't get to the Welcome screen

Your computer saves the configuration information from the last time it was booted successfully, so you may be able to boot the computer using that configuration.

1 Use the Power button to reboot the computer.

2 As soon as you hear the boot process begin, press F8 on the keyboard repeatedly.

F8

3 Select Last Known Good Configuration.

Last Known Good Configuration (your most recent settings that worked)

4 If the boot process completes successfully, great! If not, see 'Boot with Safe mode (and then reboot)', Chapter 6.

! ALERT: Sometimes, the last known good configuration isn't that great. It may boot, but with errors. If the computer boots but you aren't satisfied with the results, continue troubleshooting.

 HOT TIP: If at first you don't succeed, try, try again. It may take some finesse to press F8 at just the right time.

Problem 8: I've rebooted my computer, modem and router, but I still can't connect to the internet

You already know that the Action Center offers troubleshooting wizards (Chapter 2) and there's one there to help you resolve networking problems. However, there's also the Network and Sharing Center. This option is easier to use than the Action Center and you can open it right from the taskbar's Notification area.

1 Click the Network icon on the taskbar.

2 Click Open Network and Sharing Center.

3 If you see a red X, click it.

4 Follow the prompts to resolve the problem.

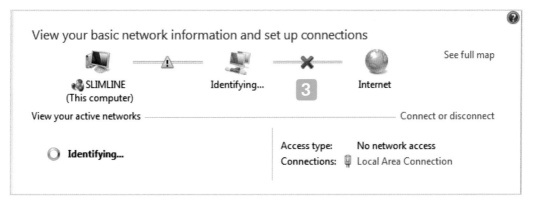

 DID YOU KNOW?

You may not see what's shown here. You may simply see your computer, an internet icon and a red X. Either way, a red X means there's a problem.

HOT TIP: You may be able to connect to resources on your local network while not being able to connect to the internet. If that's the case, call your ISP to see whether there's an outage in your area.

Problem 9: I can't afford an anti-virus program, so my computer is unprotected

There's a free program available from Microsoft called Security Essentials. It's an anti-virus program. If you don't have an anti-virus program already, get this one!

1 Visit www.microsoft.com/security_essentials/.

2 Click Download Now.

3 Look for a dialogue box similar to this one and click Run. (You may have IE8 and we're using IE9.)

4 Work through the installation process.

5 Once installed, scan your system, get updates and perform other tasks as prompted.

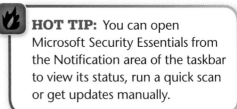

HOT TIP: You can open Microsoft Security Essentials from the Notification area of the taskbar to view its status, run a quick scan or get updates manually.

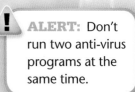

ALERT: Don't run two anti-virus programs at the same time.

Problem 10: I am getting errors that I'm low on memory

If you are receiving errors stating you're low on memory, close all open programs except the ones you need at that moment, then limit the programs that run in the background with the System Configuration tool.

1 Click Start and type msconfig.

2 Click msconfig in the results.

3 Click the Startup tab.

4 Deselect programs you installed but don't use each day, such as QuickTime, Adobe Reader, iTunes and others.

5 Click OK and restart your PC.

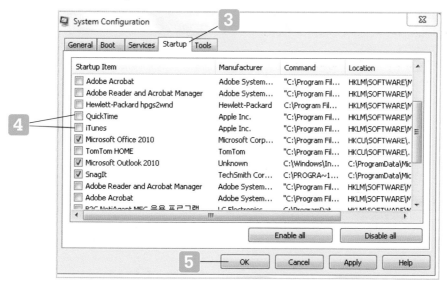